MW00532301

BEYOND A BAKE SALE

BEYOND
A BAKE SALE

HOW TOMORROW'S STUDENTS
CAN CREATE CHANGE THROUGH
ENTREPRENEURSHIP

EMILY YUAN

NEW DEGREE PRESS

COPYRIGHT © 2020 EMILY YUAN
All rights reserved.

BEYOND A BAKE SALE
How tomorrow's students can create change through entrepreneurship

ISBN   978-1-64137-378-4 *Paperback*
           978-1-64137-296-1 *Kindle Ebook*
           978-1-64137-297-8 *Digital Ebook*

CONTENTS

———

"The best way to predict the future is to create it."

—PETER DRUCKER

ACKNOWLEDGMENTS

Before getting into this book, I would like to extend a huge thank you to everyone who helped me along this journey of writing *Beyond a Bake Sale*.

First, thank you to my family for supporting me throughout the entire process and for dealing with hours of me just locking myself in my room writing. Katie, thanks for giving me feedback on my book from a high schooler's perspective!

While writing this book, I was able to have many great conversations about social entrepreneurship with many incredible people, so to everyone who took the time to either chat with me or answer questions: you have played a huge part in filling this book with fun stories and useful insights.

Thank you to all my friends who cheered me on and gave me advice as I wrote this book. A special thank you to everyone for their feedback on my cover (especially Tai)!

Finally, a HUGE thank you everyone at New Degree Press. Eric—for inspiring me to write a book, something I had never even dreamed about doing. Brian, thank you for jumping on calls with me countless times to figure out any problems I had, whether about marketing or creating a video or the cover. Kirk and Maylon, you guys are AMAZING and definitely helped me find the right direction with my book. Myriad other people and fellow authors at New Degree Press also helped me along this journey, so I want to extend this thank you to all of you.

I would also like to recognize anyone I haven't named in this section; none of this process would have been possible without you, so thanks for being awesome!

INTRODUCTION

As I kid, I wanted to change the world. I mean, who didn't? You believe you can do anything. As you get a bit older, though, reality kicks in. You realize solving world hunger isn't as easy as your seven-year-old self made it out to be. Still determined to make a difference, you settle on doing small acts of good here and there—helping at a food bank, volunteering at a homeless shelter, or the classic fundraising strategy: organizing a bake sale.

***

Currently, especially among students, everyone is volunteering. Schools are requiring it, parents are pushing their kids to do it, companies encourage employees to do it.

All sorts of programs mandate volunteering hours.

About 1/3 of all high school students volunteer at least once per month.

That said, what's with all the hype about volunteering? If we step back and reflect, three main reasons explain why most students volunteer:

1. You want to help other people.
2. It can lead to personal growth.
3. It'll look good on a resume or CV.

While these three motives are all legitimate, volunteering may not always be the best way to drive these results.

When I look back at the innumerable hours I spent baking, decorating, packaging, and selling all sorts of pastries at fundraisers, I began to wonder: what actually came out of all that time spent? Most fundraisers help raise money for some large organization, so you are definitely having some sort of impact. However, if you think about the number of combined hours your team took to plan and prepare the bake sale, was there a more efficient way to use your time that would help the population you are targeting more directly? How were you able to use your personal skillset and strengths to help make a difference? Was volunteering something YOU needed to be there for, or was it something anyone can do?

***

Yes, volunteering has a positive impact on those who are less fortunate, but the real questions to ask are:

- How much of a positive effect are you having?
- Can you find another way to help that can create an even larger impact?

Just think about it. When you do that fundraiser, what exactly happens with the money you raise? Chances are, you won't see the people you are benefitting. If you really want to make a significant difference in your community or even in the world, mindlessly doing busywork and hosting bake sales are likely not the way to go. Volunteering often merely addresses the effects of a problem and doesn't really target the root cause.

Regarding the second reason—that it leads to personal growth—volunteering does help you see the world from a different perspective and make you a more generous person, but in terms of some other valuable traits and skills such as leadership, initiative, public speaking, and problem-solving, volunteering does very little. For the most part, when you volunteer, someone simply tells you to do a task, and you assist by providing labor. You stand outside distributing flyers, packing cans, or collecting donations.

But doesn't volunteering look great on resumés, even if you aren't making much of an impact? Not really. Of course, having some sort of volunteering experience paints you as a more caring and thoughtful person; however, it typically doesn't showcase much initiative on your part, since most of the time, volunteering is just doing a repetitive task assigned to you.

So, with that said, if volunteering isn't the best way to accomplish these three goals, what other options can you pursue? Volunteering is an easy way to help a community, but when you *create* something, you actually have the opportunity to improve your leadership, communication, problem-solving, and so many more qualities that will no doubt come into play later in life. Doing so will push you out of your comfort zone and allow you to truly explore how much of an impact you can make.

**

This book is designed to inspire students to think bigger and differently on volunteering; in fact, if we are smarter about how we invest time on certain causes, I'm convinced we can drive an impact tens to hundreds of times the magnitude of that from "just" volunteering.

I set out on my own personal journey to discover the power of impact and along the way was able to uncover a secret weapon many of today's best and brightest are utilizing not only to make a difference in a major way, but also to stand out. In this book I'll share from my own experience, but I also include insights from the world's top entrepreneurs, successful young businesspeople, and hundreds of articles, videos, and talks. You'll learn from entrepreneurs such as Zuckerberg, Gates, and Branson, as well as follow the paths of successful young social change-makers.

This book is full of stories, insights, and lessons such as:

- How founder Blake Mycoskie developed his idea for TOMS and took his company to new heights, all while providing shoes for millions of people around the world.
- How you can develop the habits and skills of successful entrepreneurs and businesspeople.
- How a student was able to secure major funding and partnerships by cold-calling businesses on a dare from friends.

Use this book to guide you in your journey to make a splash in your community.

One problem with how our schools approach volunteering is they repeatedly reinforce the idea that time spent = achievement. Whether you are picking up trash in the park, helping at a soup kitchen, or tutoring kids, the school simply looks at the hours you have worked and awards credit accordingly. However, what many people overlook is that spending time on an activity doesn't necessarily mean you are really accomplishing anything; you need to find a way to create *value* for your time and effort. If your goal is to effect real change in your community, creating a social venture is a direction you may want to explore.

Students already volunteer on a regular basis, so why not harness that energy to do more than just volunteer? Time is precious, making it important for you to make the most value of the time you spend helping others. If you are deciding between volunteering or binge-watching Netflix, volunteering is the way to go, but if you are an ambitious student looking to effectively use your time to accomplish something meaningful, then you are better off devoting the time you are currently using on volunteering to creating a social venture.

If you take a quick look online, you find students who have been able to accomplish incredible feats through social entrepreneurship. In an effort to improve girls' self-images, Grace Miner started Real Girls Matter, an organization that has held large statewide conferences. Joshua Williams, a thirteen-year-old, has managed to run a nonprofit, Joshua's Heart Foundation, with more than 15,000 volunteers who feed thousands of hungry individuals in Miami. These students are going beyond the typical volunteering. They are tackling real world problems, building something from the ground up, and making a huge difference in the lives of countless people.

As a student who has experienced this overemphasis on volunteering in high school and sat through event after event doing rather mundane tasks, I personally know the feeling of wasting time doing work for which I never saw the impact. While raising money for charities was a good cause, I found organizing events, establishing relationships, and creating something infinitely more fulfilling. Curious about how I could meld my interest in business with my desire to help others, I stumbled upon the idea of social entrepreneurship, which was the perfect union of exploring entrepreneurship while simultaneously creating a social impact.

I was in your shoes a few years ago. I was ambitious, wanted to help others, and volunteered at every place I could think of in the hopes of effecting a positive change.

However, despite hours upon hours of volunteering, I felt like I wasn't making a difference. I was completing tasks that nearly anyone can do, that didn't utilize my talents and my skillset to create the biggest impact possible.

Within the past ten years, social entrepreneurship—combining entrepreneurship with creating a social impact—has become increasingly popular. If you just step back and look at the world around you, you'll find it shocking how many problems our world is experiencing, from world hunger to disease epidemics to education gaps—which affect hundreds of millions of people—are still in need of being solved. Because of this quandary, social ventures come in all kinds of forms, from integrating technology with education to creating wheelchair seat cushions.

This book has everything I wish I had known about starting something that matters.

As a student, you are probably trying to juggle schoolwork, extracurriculars, a social life, and of course, sleep; if you are reading this, however, chances are you want to create a change—no matter the scale. This book compiles tips, facts, and experience from the world's top young social entrepreneurs to help guide you through the process of making a difference in your community.

Steve Jobs said it best:

"Here's to the crazy ones, the misfits, the rebels, the trouble-makers, the round pegs in the square holes ... the ones who see things differently—they're not fond of rules.... You can quote them, disagree with them, glorify or vilify them, but the only thing you can't do is ignore them because they change things ... they push the human race forward, and while some may see them as the crazy ones, we see genius, because the ones who are crazy enough to think that they can change the world, are the ones who do."

VOLUNTEERING
AND SOCIAL
ENTREPRENEURSHIP

———

At the core of any social enterprise is one essential component: a desire to create a positive change in your community.

While most of you haven't started a social venture, you are likely familiar with volunteering. You see volunteering everywhere: schools, youth groups, churches, community centers. Wherever people need help, volunteers are usually there ready to lend a hand.

Within the past few years, volunteerism has become increasingly ingrained in American culture, and people are almost expected to work together and help the less fortunate. To see how the United States' first volunteer group came about, we'll rewind a couple centuries to colonial America.

In 1730, a huge fire broke out on a ship and later spread to all the wharf warehouses, as well as some residential homes, causing massive property damage. After learning about the fire, Ben Franklin wrote an article in the *Pennsylvania Gazette* explaining why the community needed to band together and volunteer to put out local fires. The government had measures in place in case fires occurred; however, the ship fire proved that system to be unreliable. Soon after Ben Franklin's article was published, America's first fire brigade was born—citizens banding together to donate their time for the betterment of their community. The birth of volunteerism in the United States is one of Franklin's greatest legacies, and the effects still resonate in our society today.

A few decades later, we saw this community-minded attitude once again during the Revolutionary War. Despite being understaffed and undersupplied, volunteer militias formed and trained to be ready at a minute's notice, earning them the name minutemen. These groups eventually defied all expectations and became a crucial factor in America's victory.

Fast forward to the nineteenth century and you can see a greater number of people with more wealth and better living conditions, as a result of the Industrial Revolution. The wealth gap grew, however, and soon enough, the disparity between the rich and the poor factory workers was enormous. But because the wealthy had more disposable income and free time, philanthropy boomed, and nonprofit names you may recognize today, such as the Red Cross and the YMCA, formed.

Now, in the modern-day United States, almost 25% of all Americans do volunteer work, making it what some people call the "national pastime."[1]

Many research studies have shown links between helping others and various physical and mental benefits, indicating you are not only benefitting the community but also benefitting yourself as well. In 2013, JAMA Pediatrics did a randomized controlled trial on the effect of volunteering on students' cardiovascular health. One group of tenth graders volunteered weekly at an elementary school to help the students with homework, while the control group did not. After just two months, the biological markers such as interleukin-6, C-reactive protein, and cholesterol reflected better cardiovascular health in those who volunteered. Additionally, the volunteer group ended up with lower BMIs (body mass indexes) and were less stressed. Although this study was conducted on a small sample of students, it is a great indicator of the positive effect altruism has on people.[2]

When I had dinner with a social entrepreneur who has successfully distributed hundreds of thousands of radios to people in Africa, she pointed out an interesting factor that influenced her success: sometimes, nonprofits have a too "traditional" way of thinking. She emphasized that her ability

1   Rosenburg, Stephanie. 2013. "Volunteering: History Of An American Value | Engaging Volunteers." Engaging Volunteers.

2   Schreier, Hannah M. C., Kimberly A. Schonert-Reichl, and Edith Chen. 2013. "Effect Of Volunteering On Risk Factors For Cardiovascular Disease In Adolescents." JAMA Pediatrics 167 (4): 327.

to think like an entrepreneur and a businesswoman helped her overcome many issues she faced.

As you can see, volunteering is awesome. However, while volunteering comes with health benefits and a positive community impact, you can create an even bigger splash by starting a social venture.

WHAT IS SOCIAL ENTREPRENEURSHIP?

———

Before we dive into the specifics of social entrepreneurship and how and why you should jump on this train as a student, let's get a clear definition of what entrepreneurship even is. You see the billion-dollar tech startups from Silicon Valley, but you often overlook the vast majority of startups that end up unsuccessful and fail. With entrepreneurship, the potential huge returns come with a huge risk as well. Harvard Business School professor Howard Stevenson defined entrepreneurship as "the pursuit of opportunity without regard to resources currently controlled."[3]

Now, when you tack "social" onto this definition of entrepreneurship, you add ambitious attempts to create an impact on your community. A social enterprise is a fairly broad term that applies to many different types of companies—including both for-profit and nonprofit organizations.

---

3   "'What's An Entrepreneur?' Here's The Best Answer Ever." 2020. *Inc.Com.*

A nonprofit organization and a social enterprise have fundamental differences in their business structures. Nonprofit organizations typically rely heavily on private and governmental funding in order to operate, and then invest all profits back into promoting a certain cause. Social enterprises, however, are typically for-profit organizations that work to tackle social, cultural, or environmental issues. A key item here is that social ventures should be self-sustaining and not depend on donations as their primary source of funding. For example, while nonprofits will often fundraise and apply for various grants, many social enterprises develop a product that targets a specific problem in society.

***

Matthew Goldstein began volunteering at a local weather office during major storms and was able to use what he learned there to create the social venture Emerging Response. While he was a graduate student at MIT in 2009, Matt spent a significant amount of time compiling weather data in Boston when he noticed something interesting. Each city's emergency operations center had a person dedicated to relaying the status of emergency responders to other agencies.

Surprised no centralized system existed, Matt got his idea for a startup: a software that automatically reports information about emergencies to nearby agencies so other emergency responders can be better prepared. For example, if a big gust of wind comes through a city a couple miles south of Boston, the system detects this weather event, and responders and emergency managers in Boston will know to expect power outages and prepare to respond to those issues.

***

Community service is no new concept, yet social enterprises are a relatively new phenomenon. Over half of all Canadian and American social enterprises were founded within the last six years, while almost 90 percent of India's social enterprises were founded in the last decade.[4] This indicates the social entrepreneurship sphere is rapidly evolving and lacks any dominating social ventures. You'll find no better time to jump into this field and creatively tackle pressing issues you are passionate about.

This idea of social entrepreneurship was brought to mainstream attention by one man: Bill Drayton. He has been recognized by numerous organizations as a visionary and dubbed the godfather of social entrepreneurship. As a student at Harvard University, Drayton started Ashoka, a nonprofit that has supported, and continues to support, thousands of social entrepreneurs. This organization essentially jump-started the concept of fusing innovation with social good.

***

We have all heard the proverb that goes, roughly: "You give a poor man a fish and you feed him for a day. You teach him to fish, and you give him an occupation that will feed him for a lifetime." However, Drayton explained social entrepreneurs to take this a step further, asserting that they "are not content just to give a fish or teach how to fish. They will not rest until

---

4   "Huffpost Is Now A Part Of Verizon Media." 2020. *Huffpost.Com.*

they have revolutionized the fishing industry." And that is exactly what many social entrepreneurs went on to do.[5]

In fact, you see products and services created by social entrepreneurs all around you. After witnessing children suffering from health issues due to a lack of proper footwear while he was traveling in Argentina, Blake Mycoskie formed TOMS (that's right. The founder of TOMS' name isn't Tom). For every pair of shoes purchased, TOMS gives a child a pair of shoes, resulting in the organization donating over 60 million pairs of shoes.

Before starting TOMS, Mycoskie helped out these kids in need of shoes by reaching out to his friends and family, with a pretty high degree of success. However, he knew this practice was not a sustainable way to provide shoes. Charities require the occasional donation from a caring individual, but how do you ensure a steady stream of money? By turning to entrepreneurship. Mycoskie harnessed his past business experience to create a shoe business he dubbed TOMS: Tomorrow's Shoes.

He immediately faced rejection. After coming up with the idea, he visited a local shoemaker to explain his design: a comfortable yet trendy shoe inspired by the Argentinian alpargata; however, he was called crazy and laughed at. A couple rejections later, he found someone willing to make the shoes, and TOMS was born.

The company got its big break that summer. Mycoskie began to email and call stores to see if they would be interested in

---

5   "William Drayton." 2020. *Ashoka | Everyone A Changemaker.*

selling the product, but then realized that, while he could try that in his free time, in-person meetings were infinitely more effective.

"One of the first of many important lessons I learned along the way: No matter how convenient it is for us to reach out to people remotely, sometimes the most important task is to show up in person."

TOMS was featured in the *LA Times* and *Vogue*, making the brand explode in popularity. Delivery was backed up for months, yet only one person canceled their order because of the long wait required. That first summer, the company was able to sell over 10,000 shoes. What did this success mean? People are buying into the concept, not the actual physical product.[6]

Social entrepreneurship does not have to come in the form of a product either: Muhammad Yunus started Grameen Bank, which helps people living in poverty become self-sufficient by making small loans that don't require collateral and are thus much more accessible to a larger population. These loans give them enough money to start small businesses or get on their feet when they cannot get a loan from a traditional bank. Yunus not only brought in a net income of $10 million from this project but also won the Nobel Peace Prize for helping to "create economic and social development from below." As of 2009, Grameen Bank has been able to provide microloans

---

6   "The TOMS Story | TOMS®." 2020. *Toms.Com.*

to over 10 million people in Africa, the Americas, Asia, and the Middle East. 7

If you ever look on the side of a shampoo bottle or makeup container, you may see the TerraCycle logo, which was founded by Princeton dropout Tom Szaky. TerraCycle recycles and repurposes used items and donates two cents for each item recycled. This idea blossomed into a multimillion-dollar business that is not only profitable but also makes a positive impact on society.

As you can see from several of the examples above, social entrepreneurship is a great way to pursue business while at the same time accomplishing social good.

∗∗∗

TAKEAWAYS:

- Volunteering is great and has many benefits for you personally and for your community, but social entrepreneurship will help you make an even bigger positive impact.
- Social entrepreneurship is basically altruistic entrepreneurship: you make money and do good at the same time.
- You can execute a social venture in many different ways—do some research and see what model works best for the cause you support.

---

7   "Grameen Bank." 2020. *Grameen Bank—Bank For The Poor.*

WHY YOU CAN'T DEPEND ON YOUR SCHOOL TO TEACH YOU ENTREPRENEURSHIP

The aspects of becoming an entrepreneur are many and crucial: leading and creating a company, thinking creatively, adjusting to consumer needs, and more. However, these skills are quite different from the memorizing and regurgitating that serve as the focus of many school curricula. While rote memorization may prepare students well for standardized testing and final exams, the skills we learn in school often do not overlap much with those needed to be a successful entrepreneur.

Schools do not give you the real-life experience needed to become an entrepreneur, so you must seek it out yourself. When you are in a classroom, everything is mostly confined within those limits. You have projects, papers, and presentations, but never really the opportunity to go out and try out a cool idea you have. Because of these limitations, most graduating students are set to either go off to college or work a job that requires little initiative or creative thinking on their part.

Contrary to popular belief, you don't need to be "book smart" to be a successful entrepreneur. What matters more is your ability to create and persist through any challenges thrown your way. When you pursue entrepreneurship, you will create, fail, and then recreate something infinitely better. However, this way of thinking is contradicted in the way our schools teach. When it comes to tests, assignments, and standardized testing, we are taught we need to do well each time, with even just one large slip being able to completely ruin a grade.

Entrepreneurs need to be both risk takers and individuals who seek opportunities. It requires practical skills and knowing how to apply something you learn in class to solve a real world problem.

OPINION FROM STANFORD PROFESSOR TINA SEELIG

Professor Seelig from Stanford University shared her opinion about the need for schools to teach students entrepreneurship. Because our current education system does not prepare students for starting their own ventures, many people believe entrepreneurship is an innate trait in people. She puts the process to innovation and entrepreneurship in an interesting and beautiful way:

"Imagination is envisioning things that don't exist. Creativity is applying imagination to address a challenge. Innovation is applying creativity to generate unique solutions. Entrepreneurship is applying innovations, scaling the ideas by inspiring others' imagination."

Through her many years of teaching at Stanford, Professor Seelig asserts that entrepreneurship is just like any other skill—it can be learned and mastered. The main difference between entrepreneurship and something such as learning a sport or how to play the piano is the skills that make someone a successful innovator and entrepreneur are often hard to measure. Because our school system is so focused on quantitatively measuring things, our current teaching methods don't lend themselves to learning entrepreneurial skills. It is difficult to put a "value" on how good an idea is, and it is nearly impossible to create a standardized test to see if someone is a good entrepreneur.[8] William Bruce Cameron eloquently notes that, "Not everything that can be counted counts, and not everything that counts can be counted." Entrepreneurship is a perfect example of the latter.

WHAT YOU CAN DO
Many opportunities to develop one's entrepreneurial skills exist outside venue of classroom learning. Many schools have clubs dedicated toward business and entrepreneurship such as DECA and FBLA. These clubs can help you hone your speaking skills and ability to quickly think creatively. If your school doesn't have one of these clubs, you can always

---

8   "Why It'S Imperative To Teach Entrepreneurship". 2020. *Medium*.

start an "innovation club" or talk to the school and the state chapter of DECA or FBLA to start up one of these chapters.

SOME FUN ACTIVITIES TO HELP BOLSTER YOUR ENTREPRE- NEURIAL SKILLS

Of course, you should prioritize creating your social venture, but when you have time and want to better develop your entrepreneurial skills, get together with some friends and do a few of these exercises.

$5 challenge

The $5 challenge can be done as part of a club, class, or just with a group of friends. Basically, you start out with $5, and within a certain agreed upon time span, you try to increase the value of that $5 as much as possible. This challenge was first created by a Stanford professor, who challenged his students to get into groups and make as much money as possible from the $5 in just two hours. The winning teams generated hundreds of dollars in profit through relatively simple tasks. However, most interestingly was these did not even use the $5. They realized such a small amount of money limited their ideas, so instead, turned to creativity to find a way to earn money from nothing.

One group took advantage of the long lines at popular restaurants in their neighborhood and set up a method to help those who did not want to wait in lines. Earlier that day, members of the team booked reservations at multiple restaurants in the area. That night, they went out and sold the reservations for $20 to people who did not want to wait in line. By doing this, the team managed to raise over $600.

Another team took a different approach and found a company willing to pay them $650 to advertise the company to the class. As you can see, with a little creativity, just a few dollars can go a long way.

Conquer your fears

Fear holds everyone back. Many people fear being judged by others, and because of this, aren't willing to make bold moves that often define good entrepreneurs.

Write a bucket list of things that you want to do, but never had the guts to do. Now each week, do whatever possible to cross on item off this list. Some people who have done this have been able to accomplish some pretty amazing and fun things.

In 2006 a group of four friends got together to make a bucket list of one hundred things they wanted to do before they died. They were fed up with the boredom in their everyday lives and decided to do something different. However, what initially began as a two week trip became a ten-year journey that they are still on today. The challenge and its name were inspired by a one-hundred-fifty-year-old poem by Matthew Arnold—"The Buried Life."

"...But often, in the world's most crowded streets,
But often, in the din of strife,
There rises an unspeakable desire

After the knowledge of our buried life..."

The rules for the challenge were simple: they had to come up with a list of things they would want to do assuming they had unlimited time, money, and connections. This list of things ranged from grabbing a beer with Prince Harry to playing basketball at the White House with Obama (this happened a couple years ago). Now, with the help of countless people who reached out to them, they were able to cross off almost all the items on their list. They escaped from a deserted island, crashed a party at the Playboy Mansion, went on *Oprah*, wrote a #1 New York Times Bestseller, made a successful TV show, and so much more. While embarking on this journey, the four men inspired millions of others around the world to achieve their dreams.[9]

Looking back, it is hard to imagine all this success came from a simple one-hundred-item bucket list and a desire to achieve as much as they can with their life. To be a successful entrepreneur, you need to be able to step outside of your comfort zone.

LEARN

In addition to all the knowledge you learn in classes, there is a great deal you can learn to become a better entrepreneur. One important thing to do is to keep up with current events. Especially if you want to start a social venture, you should be very aware of the world around you, particularly how it pertains to the issue you are targeting. Being well acquainted

---

9   "The Buried Life". 2020. *The Buried Life*.

with the news will not only give you more insight into your own startup but also will allow you to hold a conversation with other entrepreneurs or investors.

There are several great magazines you can read to learn more about entrepreneurship:

- *Entrepreneur*
- *Fortune Small Business*
- *Inc.*
- *Fast Company*
- *Harvard Business Review*
- *Forbes*
- *TechCrunch*
- *Wall Street Journal*
- *Wired*
- *Money*

In addition to having print magazines, nearly all these business and entrepreneurial magazines have online sites which provide interesting articles and resources. If you look up magazines pertaining to a specific sector you want to enter, chances are you can find something there.

When you have time, research a couple social enterprises to see how they run. When reading about other companies, make sure you don't read about just the ones that succeed. In an interview with Corrine, she emphasized the need not to focus solely on the successes, but also the failures. This will keep you from making the same mistakes others have made in the past.

If you have some time and want to take a course about entrepreneurship, Coursera and EdX are great places to start; they offer courses from professors at top universities and give you the option of taking the course for credit or for a certificate.

WHAT IT TAKES TO BE AN ENTREPRENEUR

When someone mentions an entrepreneur, what image comes to mind?

Chances are, you're thinking of the same type of person I am: an extroverted, articulate person who perhaps created a company out of a garage. When you take the Myers-Briggs personality test online, there is a personality type labeled as "entrepreneur"—ESTP—someone extroverted, spontaneous, and willing to take risks.

However, after speaking to and hearing the stories of successful entrepreneurs, it became clearly evident there isn't one defined personality that dictates entrepreneurial success, or even a typical linear path to becoming the CEO of the next big startup. Sarah Nahm is the CEO of Lever, a software that helps employers increase diversity in their hiring in order to create a better and more diverse workplace culture. She attended Stanford, however, didn't study anything related to business or entrepreneurship. Instead, she graduated with a degree in design, worked at a big tech company for a bit, and was one of the co-founders and the head designer of Lever. Her co-founder was the perfect embodiment of the entrepreneur stereotype and was initially the CEO of the company. However, after some time, he suggested Sarah had the knowledge and skillset to be a good CEO, which led to her eventually leading the company.

Another entrepreneur with a pretty nonlinear path is Srin Madipalli, founder and CEO of Accomable. Before going into what the company does, we need to learn a little more about Srin—he was born with spinal muscular atrophy, making him wheelchair bound his entire life. As a result, whenever he travels, he needs to find disability and wheelchair friendly housing. Hotel and lodging websites have indicators for disability friendly; however, these indicators are often incorrect, leaving disabled individuals with inaccessible lodging. Frustrated by his personal experiences, Srin started a project, Accomable, to double check the accuracy of disability accessibility at hotels. The company eventually grew, and was acquired by Airbnb, the peer to peer housing site. His journey to becoming an entrepreneur was interesting too; he studied genetics in university, became a corporate lawyer, then decided he didn't want to be a lawyer and went back to school to get his MBA. He then taught himself how to code and then sold his first startup before age 35.

Basically, the moral of the story here is you don't need to be any specific personality type to become successful as an entrepreneur; just find a cause about which you are passionate and fully commit to it!

TAKEAWAYS:
- The skills you learn in school won't always help you with entrepreneurship. However, there are many things you

can take initiative in to develop the skillset needed to be a successful entrepreneur.

- – $5 challenge
- – Create a bucket list
- – Read

- There isn't a set, linear path or personality needed to become an entrepreneur.

HOW SUCCESSFUL
ENTREPRENEURS DO IT

Think for a moment about the skills you see as important for future success...what type of traits do you come up with? Chances are the things on the top of your list aren't related to how quickly you can solve a calculus problem or how well you can recall the dates of each Civil War battle. Actually, these life skills greatly overlap with the skillset needed to become a great entrepreneur.

LifeHack, a company dedicated to helping people lead more productive and fulfilling lives, put together a list of ten things that many people regard as the most important life skills[10]:

- Organizational Skills
- Negotiation Skills
- Strong Communication Skills
- Emotional Intelligence

---

10 "10 Key Characteristics Of A Successful Entrepreneur". 2020. *Lifehack*.

- Critical Thinking
- Focus
- Teamwork
- Balance
- Confidence
- Ability to do Research

Interestingly, many of these traits overlap with the skills you develop through entrepreneurship, making entrepreneurship a great way to achieve personal growth. After interviewing and researching many entrepreneurs, I compiled a list of habits and traits these entrepreneurs thought were essential to their success.

PASSION

"A person can succeed at almost anything for which they have unlimited enthusiasm."

—CHARLES SCHWAB

"When you believe in something the force of your convictions will spark other people's interest and motivate them to help you achieve your goals. This is essential to success."

—RICHARD BRANSON

This is notably one of the most important traits for an entrepreneur to have. Most entrepreneurs are grounded by a sense of purpose, and a genuine passion for something can be sensed by both customers and investors, making it a defining variable in the success or failure of a startup.

However, *Forbes* notes that the passion doesn't have to be solely for the product. The passion can be for simply being an entrepreneur, helping other people, or creating an impact; however, some form of passion is essential to both visibly showing the appropriate enthusiasm for your business, as well as creating a mindset that allows you to persist through challenges. 11 Steve Jobs wasn't passionate about building computers; he was passionate about creating a way for people to unleash their inner creativity. He famously said, "Apple's core value is that we believe that people with passion can change the world for the better." Howard Schulz, Starbucks CEO, isn't passionate about coffee; he is passionate about creating an experience: "a third place between home and work."

Mike Kappel, the CEO of Patriot Software, explains how he was able to develop a passion for his product despite not having much initially. He and his partners wanted to create a business that allows for top executive recruiters to share information. Although Kappel did not immediately express a passion for this idea, he did have a passion for making his business succeed. He was passionate about being his own boss. This mindset allowed him to eventually develop a passion for his software and ultimately resulted in his business's success.[12]

However, while passion is good, there are things you should watch for if you are very passionate about your startup. A 2009 research study explores both the positive and negative effects of passion on startup success. While the benefits of

---

11   "5 Tips To Help You Find Your Passion". 2020. *Forbes.Com.*

12   "Executive Team | Patriot Software". 2020. *Patriot Software.*

being passionate about your startup are pretty evident, the most glaring negative is that sometimes, when you are too passionate about your idea, you are blinded to the issues that come along with it. You need to be able to scrap an idea and come up with a new one if it doesn't seem to be effective.

According to the study, entrepreneurial identities can be grouped into three types:

1. the inventor identity—liking to identify and solve problems
2. the founder identity—wanting to create a company to commercialize and exploit opportunities
3. the developer identity—passion to growing and expanding a company once it has been established

When it comes to creating a startup, figuring out exactly what you are passionate about allows you to better understand your strengths and weaknesses. For example, if you have the inventor mentality and like to create things, you would be really great at coming up with new ideas in the beginning, but you may begin to lose a bit of interest further down the line and be tempted to branch off and create new solutions for new problems.

IT IS OKAY TO FAIL, BUT MAKE SURE YOU KNOW WHY SO YOU LEARN FROM IT

"I suppose the secret to bouncing back is not only to be unafraid of failures but also to use them as motivational and learning

tools. There's nothing wrong with making mistakes as long as you don't make the same ones over and over again."

—RICHARD BRANSON

"The brave may not live forever—but the cautious do not live at all!" "Success is not final; failure is not fatal."

—WINSTON CHURCHILL

Schools do not teach you this: you will fail and get rejected—many times—and it is perfectly okay to do so. In fact, successful entrepreneurs embrace failure as a part of everyday life. The important thing is knowing what went wrong and adjusting your plan because of it.

When you are putting an incredible amount of effort into your startup, you must keep in mind that you probably will fail, and it might even end up being a good thing. In 2016, Xiaodong Lin-Siegler of Columbia University did a research study regarding student attitudes toward failure and how it impacted success. She placed high school science students into two groups. The first group learned about the failures of famous scientists such as Einstein and Curie in addition to their accomplishments, and the second group learned only about their successes. Through this study, Lin-Siegler found those who learned about the failures were more motivated and received better grades, highlighting the effect of mindset on success.[13]

---

13   "Sharing Research On Failure And Education Globally". 2020. *Teachers College—Columbia University.*

Jeff Bezos is a great example of an insanely successful entrepreneur. He built Amazon from a small online bookstore into the world's largest online retailer. While you see Amazon's success, that success was not without, and partially the result of, a string of failures throughout the company's lifespan. Perhaps one of Amazon's most significant failures is the Amazon Fire Phone. This attempt to create a phone caused Amazon to burn through over $170 million. Despite this failure, Amazon bounced back and learned to focus its products on the customer.

"Speed matters in business. Many decisions and actions are reversible and do not need extensive study. We value calculated risk taking."

—AMAZON

Real estate entrepreneur, Barbara Corcoran, came up with an idea in the 1990s to sell video tapes of salespeople introducing homes as a marketing tactic. These tapes would then be sold for $20 each and would contain all the information a person would want to know about a piece of real estate. She thought she was onto the next big thing, so she invested $71,000 in hiring professional photographers to do the filming. However, upon implementation, she realized there were major flaws in her idea, causing the entire idea to essentially flop.

Later that year, she found out about the "Internet," a new concept at the time. She created a site and posted the videos on the website and voila! The Corcoran Group became one of the first companies to post real estate listings and information on the Internet.[14]

In order to achieve great things, you must aim high and risk failure. If you only fly under the radar and stick to your comfort zone, you'll unlikely be able to make significant change.

Some things you can do:

- "One of the biggest secrets to success is operating inside your strength zone but outside of your comfort zone." —Ralph Heath
- Keep in mind, being able to accept failure and aiming big doesn't mean to aim recklessly. Take reasonable risks. Always push yourself to step outside of what you are used to but ensure whatever you are doing makes sense.
- If you haven't before, give watching some motivational videos and reading motivational books a try. Sometimes, they can be all you need to spark a bout of productivity that can keep you going.
- Whenever something doesn't go as planned, analyze it. What went wrong? What should you do next time to avoid making the same mistake? This can applied to anything: conversation with others about your idea, emails, phone calls, investment choices, etc.
- Improve your confidence and self-esteem.

In addition to setting yourself up to decrease the likelihood of you failing, practice dealing with failure! Do things you know you'll fail in to get yourself in a better mental state

---

14 "Barbara Corcoran Official Website". 2020. *Barbara Corcoran.*

when it comes time for you to deal with actual failure. There is actually a book called *The Fuckup Book*, which teaches you how to well, fuck up. They have a free pdf of the book online and it is really fun to read through (and try out the activities), so if you have twenty minutes to spare, give it a shot; you won't regret it. One of the neat exercises for getting over fears is to write out your top twelve fears and each month, get over one of them.

INVEST IN YOURSELF

A big mistake people make is only investing in your business, when it is just as, if not more crucial, to invest time and resources into yourself. Businesses can grow and crash, but time and effort taken to improve your personal skill set will be permanent. Try to do whatever you can to expand your business, entrepreneurial, and personal knowledge, as well as your mental well-being. Some ways you can work to bolster your personal skillset daily are:

- Read! As explained in the next section, reading is one of the best ways to learn in your free time.
- "Most folks are as happy as they make up their minds to be."—Abraham Lincoln. Working on a startup is a lot of work and has lots of ups and downs but try to stay positive and motivated throughout the entire process.
- Push yourself to step out of your comfort zone and try new things. This will help you grow and become more confident.
- Attend relevant workshop and seminars. If you can't find any that are convenient to go to in person, watch some *TED Talks* online when you're bored.

- Online classes. Platforms such as Khan Academy and Coursera offer online courses from professors at leading universities mostly at no cost.
- Make sure that you stay healthy as well. Exercise a couple of times a week, get in those few extra hours of sleep, and try to eat healthy.

Keep in mind—not everything you do or learn will be helpful, but more often than not, you'll derive some value from it.

Another factor that can play a large role in success is having a growth mindset, something Stanford Professor Carol Dweck spent much time researching.

Do you think your intelligence stems more from innate "smartness" or hard work? If you can't decide between one or the other, how would you divide the percentage impact of genetic vs. environmental factors?

If you attributed more than sixty percent of intelligence to environmental factors, you likely have a growth mindset, with the belief that through hard work and perseverance, you can always improve yourself and achieve success. Through research, scientists have found that students who think they can get smarter, if they put in the work, will likely invest more time and effort and end up becoming more successful. A study was done on seventh graders to see exactly how this mindset affects success. One group of students were taught the brain is malleable and can "grow." The other group was not taught this. The results were the first group achieved higher math grades than their counterparts in the second group. In essence, the study showed just knowing you are in control of your own success can lead to better achievement.[15]

READ

"The more that you read, the more things you will know. The more that you learn, the more places you'll go."

—DR. SEUSS

Warren Buffet gave credit to reading as one of his keys to success, Gates reads a book a week, and Elon Musk claims to know so much about rockets, because he "read a lot of books." Reading is one of the best ways for you to consistently learn, a trait of many successful businesspeople. Think about what goes into writing a book: the author condenses hundreds of hours of research, interviews, and personal experience into 300 or so pages. You are able to glean this knowledge in just the few short hours it takes to finish a book, which might change your perception of the world and teach you valuable things about business and entrepreneurship.

The two types of books are fiction and nonfiction. Fiction books have been shown to increase creativity, while nonfiction books can help inspire you and expand your entrepreneurial knowledge. NYU researchers Keith Oatley and Raymond Mar found people who read more fiction acquired higher levels of emotional intelligence, which is a great quality for entrepreneurs to have. In a separate study, they asked

---

15   "The Growth Mindset—What Is Growth Mindset—Mindset Works". 2020. *Mindsetworks.Com.*

participants to look at photos and identify what emotion the subject was feeling. Like the other study, they found those who read fiction were more often able to quickly and accurately identify these emotions.

Don't limit yourselves to books either; stay up on current events in the business world through online news articles and magazines. Regardless of what you are trying to do, it is always helpful to gain some basic industry knowledge in the area your social venture is addressing.

Additionally, you should get to know your cause very well. Make sure to do extensive research regarding any far reaching impacts it may have and know exactly how your idea/startup affects this issue. A huge mistake some people make is not knowing their issue well enough, putting time into the project, and realizing their mistake too late. Being well-read and knowledgeable of current events can help prevent you from overlooking major factors that may impact your project's success.

Good reads:

- Biographies of successful entrepreneurs such as Steve Jobs
- Any books that will help you develop a personal skill
- Articles from business sites such as *Entrepreneur* and *Forbes*
- Updates on industry trends in the area that you are working in

Instead of scrolling through Facebook or Instagram feeds, go find a book to flip through! A great way to keep on top of reading is always having some form of book on hand. iBook is great for reading while in the car or in line at a store, or even while on the plane. Audiobooks and podcasts are also perfect for passing time while traveling; there are no real excuses for not getting some learning in.

TIME MANAGEMENT

"It's not enough to be busy; so are the ants. The question is: what are we busy about?"

—HENRY DAVID THOREAU

Sometimes, it just seems there are not enough hours in a day. This is probably a feeling you are way too used to as a high school student—you have piles of homework, assignments, extracurriculars, and studying to do. How can you make time to start a social venture? It all comes down to efficiently managing your time.

- Delegate! If you are starting a social venture, you need to be a leader and create a team, meaning you can't do everything yourself. Splitting up roles and having each person focus on a specific thing is a great way to get more things done, than having everyone trying to work on everything.
- Make a to-do list: having a tangible list of everything that you need to get done will help you keep yourself accountable. Take ten minutes each night to cross things off your list and make a new list of what you want to accomplish for tomorrow. If you find that just making a list isn't enough to keep you on top of everything, create a schedule.

- Get rid of distractions: while technology is great and can even help keep you on task, it comes with a whole ton of distractions. There are plenty of apps out there you can download to limit the time you spend on time-wasting apps such as social media and force you to focus on your goals.
- Don't procrastinate. Everyone says this, but most people don't follow through. Tim Urban gave an entire *TED* Talk on how our brains are naturally wired to procrastinate. Making a schedule definitely helps with this! Finishing things (especially paperwork) early will give you time to look over it and make sure you didn't make any major mistakes.
- Find an order to doing things that works for you. Are you more productive in the morning? Or at night? Many people like to do larger items first, so they have fewer things to worry about when doing small tasks.
- Focus, get a lot done, and then take a break. Studies have shown the human brain can typically only focus for sixty to ninety minutes at a time. This is due to the natural biological rhythm of our bodies, much like the different stages in our sleep cycle. To take advantage of this, utilize high energy moments to get work done, and when you feel you are starting to get drained, take a short break to clear your mind. This way, you avoid burning out while still getting a ton of work done.
- Stay organized. Know where all your documents, forms, and materials are. The average American spends two and a half days per year looking for misplaced items—a huge time waster.
- There is always something that you could be doing; whether you are on a car ride, waiting for an appointment,

or waiting for a friend; you don't have to just sit there and do nothing or scroll through social media on your phone, you could download a few inspirational books or listen to a podcast to learn while passing time.

NETWORK

"Position yourself as a center of influence—the one who knows the movers and shakers. People will respond to that, and you'll soon become what you project."

—BOB BURG

"The richest people in the world look for and build networks, everyone else looks for work."

—ROBERT KIYOSAKI

Business involves connections. In fact, research has shown that the most successful entrepreneurs are great at networking. To successfully network, you need to be able to both develop and maintain connections with the people you meet. Even if you think you don't actively network, you should always maintain and cultivate old relationships. Networking also doesn't have to be done for the pure purpose of developing business connections; you should stay in touch with people to build relationships.

- Learn to enjoy networking. Networking is an essential part of business; while some extroverts seem to be naturals at it and love the social interaction, many people may see it as "fake" or "social climbing." Networking is just about creating more relationships with people. Instead of dreading talking to more people at a networking event, see it as an opportunity to learn, find new opportunities, and perhaps make a new friend.

- Reach out to current connections for help: for example, if you go through a friend's LinkedIn and see someone you need to get in touch with, ask your friend to introduce the two of you!
- Offer to help others.
- Find networking and entrepreneurship events. At these places, everyone who is there is looking to network and meet new people, so don't hesitate to go up and talk to people.
- Be memorable: have a quality conversation with someone as opposed to just giving them a card.
- Tell stories! Studies have shown that stories are one of the best ways to engage someone; your brain not only processes the words, but also experiences the event.
- Follow up on conversations: if you find an article relevant to a conversation you had, don't hesitate to send it over to the other person to stay engaged!
- Connect with them on social media to stay in touch: you probably have Instagram and/or Facebook and/or Snapchat. All of these are great ways to keep up with their life—drop an occasional comment or text to see how they are doing! If they are ever in town, try to get in touch and grab lunch or something of sort.

Jimmy Fallon's journey to becoming a popular TV host is a great example of networking completely changing someone's career. Surprisingly, his was a computer science major in university when he began developing an interest in comedy. His audition tape was sent to SNL, where an agent saw potential in him. Set on joining SNL, Fallon dropped out of college with just one semester left and auditioned. After joining the cast in 1998, he met the person who would change his career forever: Lorne Michaels. Micheals is the show's creator, and is regarded as quite intimidating by many people. However, the show's director liked Fallon and urged him to develop a closer relationship with Micheals and make his way into Micheals's after-parties. Soon enough, they became pretty close friends. Later on, Fallon quit SNL to give Hollywood a shot, which didn't end up going well, but his luck took a turn for the better when the position of host for the late night show opened up. Because of his great relationship with Lorne Michaels, he was able to get the position, which ended up being his big break into the industry and where he begun his rise to fame.[16]

CALL INSTEAD OF EMAIL

Despite the ease of sending an email or texting, calling is one of the quickest and most powerful way to decrease any confusion that may occur. Of course, in person meetings are ideal because they allow you to develop a much better personal connection, however, calling is a close second in its effectiveness. Emails can take days to get a response to, but with calls, you usually get your problem addressed immediately. Additionally, calling or holding a face to face meeting within your organization can improve communication and better solve any issues that may have arisen. You'll be able to actually build relationships through these calls, as opposed to sending impersonal emails.

---

16   "Jimmy Fallon". 2020. *Biography.*

There are a couple cases when you should email instead of calling:

- When there is a set of detailed written instructions that the other party needs
- When you need a record of the conversation

However, especially if the matter requires you to develop a relationship with someone, calling is a much better option. According to a study done by NYU, "many people are over-confident in their ability to accurately relay emotions when it comes to email."

Here are some tips when it comes to calling:

- If you are calling someone who you are trying to get to invest in your business, have a quick elevator pitch ready.
- Get to the point, however, still let people know why you are calling.
- Speak clearly
  - After each call, reflect on how it went. Think about what you could have said to make it better, and what direction that would have taken the conversation in. Putting more thought and reflection into these conversations will help you become a much better conversationalist.
  - If appropriate, send a follow up with a very short recap and a thank you, plus include if there is a need for any follow up calls.

Cold Calling: this may seem intimidating, but if you are able to, it may help you get more funding and more connections.

An important tip for cold calling someone is connecting with them a little beforehand and give them a heads up. If you want to talk to an entrepreneur that you admire, go like some of their posts on social media (many use Twitter a lot) and try to message them to set up a quick call. Once you get on the call, ensure that you know what you are talking about—either got through it once in your head beforehand, or jot down a list. You don't have to look at this as a task you must do, but rather, as just an opportunity to connect with more people that you can take.

DISSATISFACTION WITH THE STATUS QUO

"According to all known laws of aviation, there is no way that a bee should be able to fly. Its wings are too small to get its fat little body off the ground. The bee, of course, flies anyways. Because bees don't care what humans think is impossible."

—BEE MOVIE

"Be resilient and stay true to your vision and values. If it were easy, someone would have done it before. But if you have made the decision to take your idea and transition to the overwhelming and exhilarating path of social entrepreneurship, your idea is likely worth pursuing and you will find ways to overcome hurdles."

—SONA SHAH

When it comes to social entrepreneurship, perhaps one of the most important qualities for the founder to embody is being community driven. The end goal needs to be to create an impact in the community. You need to be dissatisfied with the status quo and have a desire to effect positive change. Creating a startup is difficult, and in order to persist through these challenges, you need to truly care about the cause your company is focusing on. Duke's Center for Advancement of Social Entrepreneurship found that most social entrepreneurs had a healthy impatience with the way things are. They are frustrated at the bureaucracy and lack of political will that impede positive social change.

Sam Polk was living a pretty successful life; he graduated from Columbia University and went on to work as a trader on Wall Street. However, a couple of years into the job, he began to develop a better idea of all the greed and corruption occurring in society and was inspired to "create a more equitable world for all."[17]

In 2013, he founded GroceryShips, a social venture which aims to help people of all income levels have access to nutritious and healthy foods. In many impoverished communities, fast food is the only affordable option, which can lead to a much higher rate for many diseases in these neighborhoods. GroceryShips helps solve this problem by raising funds and then providing high quality meals priced on a sliding scale, thereby making these healthy meals affordable for all.

17   "How Sam Polk, Former Wall Street Trader And 'Wealth Addict,' Broke Free Of His Golden Handcuffs". 2020. *Forbes.Com*.

BEING ABLE TO NETWORK AND CONNECT WITH PEOPLE

Building a strong professional network is crucial to providing opportunities that would have never been available otherwise. You'll be able to chat with and receive advice from people who have already been successful in achieving something like what you are trying to do. If you don't have one already, consider getting a LinkedIn account, the professional version of social media.

Networking can help you connect with people who can help you along the way or know someone who can. It is extremely important to try to *connect* with the people you meet and interact with each one. You need to get to know that person, and make sure they remember you as well. Several things you can do to develop a closer relationship with people you meet are:

- Be interested in them! Be curious in what they are working on. Talk to them about their idea, and perhaps even offer some helpful input. You should make sure you are developing a genuine interest in the people with whom you are trying to connect.
- Follow up with them regularly. If appropriate, occasionally check in to see how they are doing. When the holidays come around, send them a card (or an e-card).
- Help them out with something. Humans inherently adhere to the concept of reciprocity. If you do something nice for someone, he or she will be inclined to return the favor. If you know someone who they could talk to that would benefit their business, give them their contact information! It never hurts to be as helpful as possible, so make sure you do this!

INTROVERTS VS. EXTROVERTS

If you've ever taken the Myers-Briggs personality test, which gives you four letters that supposedly help define your personality type, you probably noticed there was a specific combination called the "entrepreneur" personality—ESTP. The E in the sequence stands for extroversion, which makes you wonder: do extroverts have a better shot at creating a successful startup?

Extroverts are people who derive energy from being around others, while introverts need time alone to recharge. Most people fall somewhere in the middle of this spectrum and are called ambiverts.

Being more outgoing and social, extroverts tend to have larger networks they can reach out to, which is definitely a plus when it comes to entrepreneurship. Additionally, extroverts tend to be a bit more personable, which can make them appear as more effective team leaders. However, all this time spent socializing may get in the way of focusing and getting work done, which are qualities that are beneficial to introverts.

When it comes to entrepreneurship, you find both extroverts and introverts successfully running the enterprise, so it doesn't really matter which one you are; if you can focus and create the right connections and network, you are already on your way to success.

Bill Gates, the founder of Microsoft and a billionaire entrepreneur said:

"Well, I think introverts can do quite well. If you're clever you can learn to get the benefits of being an introvert, which might be, say, being willing to go off for a few days and think about a tough problem, read everything you can, push yourself very hard to think out on the edge of that area. Then, if you come up with something, if you want to hire people, get them excited, build a company around that idea, you better learn what extroverts do, you better hire some extroverts, like Steve Ballmer I would claim as an extrovert, and tap into both sets of skills in order to have a company that thrives both as in deep thinking and building teams and going out into the world to sell those ideas."

This of course, ties back to being able to make a great team that complements your skills, which is explained in a later chapter.

NEGOTIATING

In business (and in life), you will have to negotiate for many different things. These can range from small compromises and resolving internal team conflicts to settling business deals. A *Harvard Business Review* report outlined how to walk away from a negotiation with a successful result. Below are a few of the points I thought would be the most helpful:

- Prepare: obviously, this isn't possible if you are thrown into something on the spot. Otherwise, it is always good to do your research ahead of time. Know what the other party has and is aiming to achieve.
- Set specific goals: Deborah C. Zetik and Alice F. Stuhlmacher of DePaul University conducted a research study finding that specific goals are a key element of negotiation

success saying, "I would like to increase the rate by x%" is better than just saying "I'll try my best."

- Report losses in one big chunk but deliver good news in stages: Dniel Kahneman and Amos Tversky found while people preferred to hear several small wins, they would rather hear losses all at once.
- Don't respond too quickly. While immediately responding may be a sign you are committed, it may make people think they did not ask for enough and regret their decision.
- Don't seem too excited or brag about negotiating a good deal: the other party may be less inclined to work with you in the future if you do.
- Prepare answers for the hardest questions you think will come up.
- Don't get too nervous—it shows. You can turn your anxiety into excitement, or just practice more and be comfortable with the process!

There are many great books and online resources to learn more about negotiation that go more in depth about different tactics and the psychological basis behind them. One important variable in any negotiation is the BATNA—the best alternative to a negotiated agreement. That is, if the other party doesn't take your offer, what is their next best alternative? If you know the other person's BATNA but they don't know yours, you start out with more leverage over the deal.[18]

Negotiation is a valuable skill you will inevitably use in all parts of your life—make sure you master it!

---

18 "Negotiations". 2020. *Hbr.Org.*

TRY OUT THESE HABITS!

- **Wake up early:** As tempted as you might be to sleep in until noon on weekends, most successful entrepreneurs get up early. Give it a try. You'll be surprised at how much more time you seem to have. When you get up early, you avoid the noise and commotion of everyone else being awake, which will allow you to have a few hours where you can be extra productive.

- **Don't multi-task:** People say this time and time again: your brain can't focus on multiple things at once and do them well. When you are "multi-tasking," you're not actually doing a bunch of things at once: your brain is just switching quickly between different tasks. If you try to do two important things at once (such as trying to call someone while writing an email, chances are you'll make a mistake when doing both). Instead compartmentalize and block out your schedule. Set certain time limits for tasks to keep yourself accountable for finishing them.

- **Simplify your routine:** Cut things out you don't really need to do. Think about an easier way to accomplish each thing in your schedule; doing this will save you quite a bit of time.

- **Don't forget to relax:** Many entrepreneurs burn out from the intense stress and workload. Make sure you have time to just chill, hang out with friends, and do something you love.

- **Write things down:** It's great to be able to keep things in your head, but sometimes, the best way to stay organized is to write everything down in your phone notes or in your notebook. Whether it is a schedule or just some ideas, keep a hard copy!

SOCIAL ENTREPRENEURSHIP PUT TO WORK

———

In this chapter, I have put together a compilation of interesting social ventures where you can get inspiration. Currently, there are social ventures targeting all kinds of different causes, and as mentioned before, it is vital to evaluate both successes and failures. More than half of all social enterprises die within the first five years, indicating is it not only important to see why the successful startups succeeded, but also what caused the huge number of social ventures with great ideas to fail. A huge misconception is that a great idea will automatically lead to a successful startup.

However, with billions of people in the world, chances are, someone has already thought of your idea. Merely having an amazing idea or cause will not prevent major mistakes and flaws from impeding the success of a venture. An organization's success is often as much, if not more, rooted in the execution of the idea than the actual idea itself. So, it is essential to look at other companies—what their teams look like, what their path to success was,

FLORA

Have you ever checked your weekly phone screen time and were immediately shocked by the number of hours you wasted doing pretty much nothing? There is a name for smartphone addiction: *nomophobia*—the fear of not having your phone. Studies have shown that phone overuse may lead to stress, anxiety, sleep deprivation, narcissism, and a whole slew of other issues. A team of college students decided to combat this issue by creating Flora—a multiuser productivity app that can keep you and your friends off your phone for a set number of minutes through behavioral psychology. The app's reward system can trigger a dopamine release—something typically associated with addiction. However, ironically, the thing you are getting addicted to is staying off your phone. The app lets you plant trees that require a set amount of time to grow, ranging from five minutes to two hours; however, this time must be spent off your phone. If you exit the app, the tree dies. The social impact of Flora doesn't just lie in helping people live more productive lives by breaking their phone addiction; the app offers several ways allowing you to contribute to planting real trees.

Despite the great concept and app design, Flora falls a little short in popularity to another productivity app you have heard about—Forest. Interestingly, Flora and Forest were started at the same college and worked together, with Forest being a single user productivity app and Flora focusing more in the multi-user direction. However, as it became more and more popular, Forest began to offer a multi-user option for a fee, which caused Flora to break off their relationship. The key takeaway here? While starting a company with a partner or partner company may come with a couple of benefits, many people will choose personal gain over loyalty to the partnership. Be careful!

THE SHOE THAT GROWS

In 2007, Kenton Lee, a recent college graduate, visited an orphanage in Kenya, where he came across a glaring issue that has been poorly addressed. Many of the kids in the village have no shoes. What's more, over 2 billion people in the world have a soil born disease, which is more likely to occur if a child is walking barefoot. When Lee returned from the trip, he created the nonprofit organization Because International to serve as the overarching structure for a shoe that expands as a kid's foot gets bigger. After working with a design studio, he came up with a design that would be a huge success: The Shoe That Grows. From the very beginning, Lee had a clear goal, which he expressed in an email: "We just wanted to create a shoe that can 1) grow as much as possible, 2) last as long as possible, 3) cost as little as possible." The resulting shoe looks like a sandal with a contraption on the top of the shoe which allows the shoe to expand by buckling the shoe into a different notch. While a kid may quickly outgrow a regular shoe, this design allows the $15 shoe to comfortably fit the child for four to five years, solving the problem of the high cost of replacing shoe after shoe, especially in more impoverished communities. To date, Because International has sold over 120,000 shoes to countries around the world.

A decade later, the nonprofit saw a new channel for expansion: The United States. The product was initially targeted toward third world countries; however, they began to see growing interest from the US and have begun to sell expandable shoes under the company, Grofive. When you start a social venture, you never really know what direction it will take you, and in the end, you may end up turning a large profit while still creating a great impact on society.[19]

OXY2

Statistics about the air quality around the world are horrifying. In 2015, the research group Berkeley Earth estimated that the bad air quality in China has led to 1.6 million deaths per year, proving that the increasing rate of industrialization has had severe health consequences by causing air pollution. Elvis Zhang, born in Hong Kong and who grew up mostly in Hong Kong and China, personally experienced the effects of this. When he moved to the United States for school, he began to conduct material science research to develop something to combat these negative health effects. This research led him to develop two things: a mask with a thin, passive filter, and a "passive net" technology, which can be installed on buildings and other structures to filter out pollutants from the air. He grew his company and worked with large companies such as 3M to produce and implement the products and took a gap year after high school deferring his acceptance to MIT to spend time working on Oxy2. After a couple years, Elvis sold the company so he could work on his next

19   "How The Flora App Developers Use Behavioral Psychology To Help
     Users Live Their Best Lives | Designli Blog". 2020. *Designli Blog.*

endeavor. As of March 2019, the organization has provided protection from air pollution to over 70,000 people.

Elvis is now a sophomore at Stanford and has recently used his background in research to start an investment fund focused on healthcare technology in both the Unites States and Asia. In our interview, he noted that he plans on using what he learns through investing in healthcare tech to eventually start his own tech company.

Basically, a social venture is a great learning experience that both creates a positive impact on the community and sets the foundation for future career opportunities.

KOE KOE TECH

Koe Koe Tech is a perfect embodiment of using technology to help solve a previously difficult to address problem. Since technology has been developing so quickly and has made many tasks infinitely more convenient, it has become a direction many social ventures choose to pursue. Michael Lwin & Dr. Yar Zar Min Htoo, the founders of Koe Koe Tech, strive to create software that makes healthcare more accessible to people in Myanmar. They offer a free app for maternal and childcare and have other paid software to help doctors with paper and management. With mobile phone usage soaring less developed countries, it is easier than ever to reach and help these people through technology. Their system benefits thousands of people in Myanmar, while still being for-profit, allowing Koe Koe to be more self-sustaining and have more financial freedom. However, as they began reaching more people, they realized a problem. The Burmese speaking people of Myanmar had a hard time creating a Google account to be able to download the app from the Play Store. While Koe Koe has over 100,000 people using the app, they say six times as many people attempt to download the app but are unable to due to the language barrier. Problems like these are things you should watch for and consider when conducting background research on your ideas.

Take a moment to think about the issue you want to target with your social venture, and brainstorm ways technology can be used to help solve it. Is there an app that can better connect you with your target audience? Are there any new technologies that may be relevant? Mark Meeker, an American venture capitalist, releases a yearly analysis of internet trends, which can be helpful if you decide to create an internet based startup. If you can't think of anything, ask your tech savvy friends and see if anyone can come up with anything. Technology can definitely make a huge difference in the success of your project!

REGRAINED
Recently, there has been a pretty big growth in companies that focus on reducing food waste by repurposing unwanted food. Usually, this applies to visually unappealing fruits or something of that sort; however, the two UCLA students Jordan Schwartz & Dan Kurzrock targeted an issue most people didn't even know existed—leftover grain from brewing beer. In the past, breweries have established close relationships with local farms to sell off used grain as livestock feed, but with the increased presence of urban breweries, these relationships have become harder to establish. As a result, even

a small brewery may send millions of pounds of the "spent grain," a product low in sugar and high in fiber and protein, making it difficult to use for traditional baking to the landfill each year.

However, if you think a little further, you might realize something else producers *want* to be low sugar, high fiber, and high protein: protein bars. Spotting this idea, Schwartz and Kurzrock founded Regrained, a startup focused on producing energy bars using the leftover material from brewing beer. The pair both brewed beer at UCLA, and simply wanted to have the profits from selling their baked goods to offset the cost of making beer. A bit further down the line, they began to produce what is now their primary product: protein bars.

While the company initially scraped up money from personal funds and friends and family to get by, they received a large amount of money through venture capital funding, which allowed the company to expand to stores all over the country. They are now expanding beyond their protein bars to using their "super grain" in other sweet and savory snacks. While Schwartz and Kurzrock began small, focusing only on their work at UCLA, the idea eventually grew into a product that spans the nation. As you see here, you don't have to start by wanting to change the world; try to create a change in any way possible, even if it's just in your local community. If your idea is good and you execute it properly, you will inevitably draw attention to your project that will help it grow and expand.

SIERRA NEGRA

Like many other social ventures, Leticia Gasca, a junior in college, drew inspiration for her idea from her personal experience. Ever since she was sixteen, she paid yearly visits to indigenous communities in Mexico as a part of service trips. On these trips, she began to realize how poor the conditions were; water was scarce, employment was hard to find, and the residents' makeshift homes could be easily blown away by a strong gust of wind. One thing Gasca found to be beautiful, despite the living conditions, was the embroidery made by street artisans used to supplement their income. However, a project that would have taken a month to complete would typically only sell for $2.

Determined to help these artisans, Gasca started a company when she returned home—Sierra Negra. Sierra Negra was a fair trade company providing artisans with an income much greater than they typically made by selling these handmade items in stores around the United States. Despite the good sentiment and idea, however, Gasca and her team did not create a realistic and comprehensive financial plan for the company, which ultimately led to its failure. They did not initially think of all the costs they would incur, and profited less than expected due to the low margins at which they sold to the stores. The company had won several awards for creating positive societal change; however, in the end, was not successful due to a flaw that could have been discovered early on and avoided.

CAUSE—THE PHILANTHROPUB PUB

The name is self-explanatory: Cause is a restaurant and bar that donates its profits to charity. Co-founders Raj Ratwani and Nick Vilelle came up with this idea and opened the restaurant in Washington, DC. The concept was great. In fact, the concept may have been even better than great. Before they even opened, the idea raised over $23,000 on Indiegogo to help fund supplies for the launch. The restaurant was recognized in Steven Colbert's TV show, as well as the *New York Times*, causing everyone to have high hopes for it. Initially, business was good. Lots of nonprofits and corporations booked group events at the venue, and the pub turned a positive profit. However, the buzz slowly died down, and the pub began to struggle to make money, with the two founders not even taking a salary from themselves.

The team did not realize what was wrong until it was too late. It turns out, Cause attracted many events and groups, however, didn't serve as a place for people to regularly come just to grab dinner or a drink. It was good they focused on the philanthropic aspect of the business, but what they should have also put an emphasis on is the quality of the food, which according to reviews, is not lacking. At the end of the day, you go to restaurants to eat good food, not just to contribute to a good cause. The mis-focus with Cause may have cost it its business. After the pub temporarily closed for an AC malfunction during the summer, it never opened back up.

SHEA YELEEN INTERNATIONAL

Shea Yeleen has a similar goal to Sierra Negra of providing higher paying jobs for women in rural areas. Instead of targeting indigenous communities that produce crafts in Mexico, Shea Yeleen works with individuals in West Africa to produce high quality, sustainable shea products. At the same time, the organization helps women in West Africa live more comfortably, stable lives by providing them with an income that is five times greater than the minimum wage in their country. After helping make the Shea products, Shea Yeleen helps women develop skills to become more financially independent.

The mastermind behind this entire nonprofit is Rahama Wright, someone who didn't have any background knowledge about shea butter. She was able to be so successful in her efforts to positively impact women because of the extensive research she had conducted before starting the project. In an interview, she advises anyone interested in creating a social impact to do the same thing: do a lot of research, and then tackle the issue at full speed.

CORAL VITA

Another huge issue many people are trying to address is the devastating impact of climate change. Rising carbon dioxide levels as a result of industrial growth has led to ocean acidification, which along with habitat destruction and unsustainable fishing behaviors, kills coral. Ninety percent of coral reefs are projected to be destroyed by 2050. Yale students Gator Halpern and Sam Teicher decided to tackle this issue and founded Coral Vita; a project dedicated to building a global network of coral farms to replenish this destroyed coral.

When they were first getting started, they used resources provided by their college to serve a springboard for this project. They worked on this project while still in school and were awarded a $1000 grant by Yale's entrepreneurship institute. While Halpern and Teicher each didn't have an extensive research background in coral, they reached out to professionals and got them on board, demonstrating how much help finding people more experienced than you can be. The project later went on to receive many entrepreneurship and environmental impact awards.

POLLINATE

There is quite a large portion of the Indian population who are impoverished and unable to afford basic everyday needs, as well has have no access to internet or even electricity. Pollinate aims to rectify this issue through by training "change agents," people they find to serve as a mentor to their peers. The change agents, the Pollinators, sell and distribute affordable necessities such as lights, stoves, and water filters. These items can help greatly improve a family's quality of life and working with Pollinate helps lift people out of poverty. Because these typically cost more than what a family can afford at once, Pollinate has a deferred payment option where the product can be paid for over the course of a couple weeks. If a payment doesn't come in, a Pollinator can go check on the person and see what is going on. Additionally, this not only helps the families, but also the environment, since families can use cleaner energy than the kerosene that is typically used in their communities.

The organization has been very successful, having impacted over 50,000 people in India and Bangladesh. When Pollinators revisit communities to see the impact the program has been having, there is a noticeable difference; people are using safer energy sources, and it is easier for the kids to study at night because of the solar lamps Pollinate provides.

AGRICOOL

With our rapidly growing population, food availability and sustainability are becoming increasingly important. The founders of Agricool, Guillaume Fourdinier and Gonzague Gru, kept this in mind and created a product that fits perfectly with our world's increasing globalization. Instead of growing crops using traditional methods, Agricool farms strawberries in shipping containers. This not only conserves space and allows crops to be grown where they typically would not be able to, but also gives the owner the ability to alter lighting, humidity, and temperature to cater these conditions to the specific plant. The small container conserves water and allows the crops to be grown year-round. The plants are pesticide free and organic and have been found to have higher nutrient and sugar levels than standard strawberries. Agricool is based in Paris and is set to build one hundred of these container farms by 2021. Right now, the company only grows strawberries, however, is set to expand to other crops such as tomatoes soon.

Through the most recent round of funding, Agricool raised over $28 million, giving the venture enough capital to hire more employees and build the additional container farms. While the concept seems simple, much effort goes into design and perfecting the conditions. In fact, over seventy percent of Agricool's staff is focused on R&D. While the company is rather small right now, there is serious potential for growth and expansion.

CHATTERBOX

If you have been keeping up with the news, you know the political situation around the world is displacing millions of people, leaving all these refugees with no good options of places to go. According to some studies, there will be over 50 million displaced people in the world by 2050. At the same time, there is a shortage of language specialists. Seeing this overlap, the founders created Chatterbox. Chatterbox helps give these refugees jobs as language teachers, and pay them seventy percent of the revenue in salaries. This allows the refugees to build a professional network and develop skills that can lead to future job success. Chatterbox is an online service with trained refugees as language coaches, allowing users to both develop their skill in a language and create a positive community impact. They have trained over one hundred coaches and have trained over eight hundred users in another language, showing there is quite a bit of initial momentum. Chatterbox is a great example of fulfilling a need; while at the same time, creating a social impact.

SOME KEY TAKEAWAYS

What is important to draw from these examples is social ventures can be a bit different from your typical startups. Their main purpose is bringing positive change to the community. This gives them a unique set of challenges, and while it may be easier for them to garner community support, having such a community-based focus may make it difficult to create a continuous source of revenue.

The Failure Institute conducted a study of over one hundred failed social enterprises to find the most common reasons for failure. It all boiled down to three main points:

- Not enough funding and resources: This is a problem all startups face but is even more applicable to social ventures. Many social entrepreneurs don't have the skills or experience needed to raise enough capital to run their business, which ultimately results in failure. Social ventures typically are also less attractive to investors because their main purpose is to create social change as opposed to making money.
- Context: Basically, this means the social venture was started at the wrong place at the wrong time—while the idea is great and the intention is amazing, there just isn't enough awareness about the issue in the community right now, making it difficult to garner support.
- Board of Directors: This issue is addressed in a later chapter in this book, and directly addresses this issue. When there is major conflict between the leaders of the organization, or if people show different amounts of commitment to the company, it is essential to develop a strong leadership team.

Additionally, starting a social enterprise is a great launchpad for personal growth and future growth opportunities.

ENTREPRENEURS TO KNOW

Before getting into the specifics of starting a social venture, I want to introduce you to a couple incredibly influential entrepreneurs. They not only have inspiring stories, but also often come up in conversations, so here is a brief introduction to them! This is by no means an exhaustive list, but rather, a brief introduction to just a couple people you should know!

JEFF BEZOS

Jeff Bezos is arguably one of the world's most successful entrepreneurs. Within the last 30 years, he was able to grow Amazon from a discount online bookstore into the go-to online shopping site and a muti-billion dollar company. After graduating from Princeton with a degree in electrical engineering and computer science, he went on to work on Wall Street for a couple years, before founding the company that revolutionized online shopping—Amazon. Like some other famous entrepreneurs, he founded his company out of his garage.

In addition to running Amazon, Bezos also owns the newspaper, The Washington Post, as well as Blue Origin, a company that develops rockets for commercial use.

◇◇◇◇◇◇◇◇◇◇◇◇◇◇◇◇◇◇◇◇◇◇

Tips from Jeff Bezos:[20]

Bezos not only exemplifies many ideal entrepreneurial traits, but also has posted fourteen leadership guidelines on his website, some of which will also be discussed below.

1. **FOCUS ON A LONG TERM GOAL:** During the 2000 dot-com crash, Bezos demonstrated his focus on the future of the company in his letter to shareholders: "Amazon.com today [has] the brand, the customer relationships, the technology, the fulfillment infrastructure, the financial strength, the people, and the determination to extend our leadership in this infant industry and to build an important and lasting company." In another letter, Bezos explained that all of Amazon's decisions are made with a long-term goal in mind.

2. **FAILING IS OKAY:** While you see all the success Amazon has achieved, that success was a result of a string of failures that have occurred throughout the company's lifespan. Perhaps one of Amazon's most significant failures is the Amazon Fire Phone. In fact, the phone cost Amazon around $170 million dollars. Despite this

---

20 "Jeff Bezos". 2019. *Forbes.*

failure, Amazon still bounced back and learned to focus its products on the customer. Speed matters in business. Many decisions and actions are reversible and do not need extensive study. We value calculated risk taking.

3. **CUSTOMER OBSESSION:** Leaders start with the customer and work backwards. They work vigorously to earn and keep customer trust. Although leaders pay attention to competitors, they obsess over customers. When creating your social venture, you need to focus on who your product audience is, and optimize that for that specific population as much as possible. This will ensure you are creating an impact on the intended group of people.

4. **TAKE OWNERSHIP IN CREATING CHANGE:** Leaders are owners. They think long term and don't sacrifice long-term value for short-term results. They act on behalf of the entire company, beyond just their own team. They never say, "That's not my job."

5. You need to be willing to put in the work necessary to make your social venture successful, even if it means you picking up a little from someone else's slack. If you have the mindset of "Oh that is their job, and since they're not doing it, I guess we have to wait for them," it will be difficult for you to achieve as much as you could have.

6. **LEARN AND BE CURIOUS:** Leaders are never finished learning and always seek to improve themselves. They are curious about new possibilities and act to explore them.

7. **HIRE AND DEVELOP THE BEST:** Leaders raise the performance bar with every hire and promotion. They recognize exceptional talent, and willingly move them throughout the organization. Leaders develop leaders and take seriously their role in coaching others. We work

on behalf of our people to invent mechanisms for development like Career Choice.

8. **INSIST ON THE HIGHEST STANDARDS:** Leaders have relentlessly high standards—many people may think these standards are unreasonably high. Leaders are continually raising the bar and drive their teams to deliver high quality products, services, and processes. Leaders ensure defects do not get sent down the line and that problems are fixed, so they stay fixed.

9. **THINK BIG:** Thinking small is a self-fulfilling prophecy. Leaders create and communicate a bold direction that inspires results. They think differently and look around corners for ways to serve customers.

10. **FRUGALITY:** This one is especially important for a new startup. As a student, chances are, you don't have a significant amount of resources or funding to start with, so you need to find a way to make the most out of what you have. You need to be resourceful. Accomplish more with less. Constraints breed resourcefulness, self-sufficiency, and invention. There are no extra points for growing headcount, budget size, or fixed expense.

11. **EARN TRUST:** This is a trait that is not limited to entrepreneurship, but leadership in general. In order for a leader to be successful, they need to first earn the trust of people who they are leading. You need to stay humble and connect with the people with whom you work.

12. **DIVE DEEP:** Leaders operate at all levels, stay connected to the details, audit frequently, and are skeptical when metrics and anecdote differ. No task is beneath them.

13. **HAVE BACKBONE; DISAGREE AND COMMIT:** Leaders are obligated to respectfully challenge decisions when they disagree, even when doing so is uncomfortable

or exhausting. Leaders have conviction and are tenacious. They do not compromise for the sake of social cohesion. Once a decision is determined, they commit wholly.

14. **DELIVER RESULTS:** Leaders focus on the key inputs for their business and deliver them with the right quality and in a timely fashion. Despite setbacks, they rise to the occasion and never settle.

RICHARD BRANSON

Richard Branson had dyslexia and poor grades when he was in school, and when he graduated, the headmaster told him that he would either go to prison or become a millionaire. Now, Branson is a billionaire who does not run just one billion dollar company, but eight. He founded the Virgin group when he was 20, and it now controls over 400 companies around the world.

His entrepreneurial spirit was present from a very young age. At 16, he had his first start-up success with a magazine called "Student". In just a year, his net worth as a result of this company became over $50,000. In his early 20s, he started a record store—Virgin Records. His net worth hit 5 million dollars by the time he was just 29, but his entrepreneurial journey was just beginning. He went on to found Virgin Atlantic Airlines, a railway company, and even got involved in technology for space travel.

In addition to being a successful entrepreneur, Branson is a large environmental and humanitarian advocate, pledging 3 billion dollars to environmental causes in 2006. He has published many book detailing his journey and offering advice to entrepreneurs. Recently, he create a social media post with advice for young entrepreneurs who want to start a side hustle.

◇◇◇◇◇◇◇◇◇◇◇◇◇◇◇◇◇◇◇◇◇◇◇◇◇◇◇◇◇◇

Tips from Richard Branson:[21]

1. **HAVE GRIT:** This concept is expressed by numerous entrepreneurs, and is cited by Angela Duckworth, a MacArthur Genius Fellow, in her book as a trait with one of the strongest correlations with success.
2. **START SMALL:** Branson urges students to start small, yet think big, saying that most of his companies initially started as a small idea. However, this doesn't mean you should limit your company to what it starts out as. You should always be thinking of ways to expand, grow, and better develop your business, so it can make as big an impact as possible.
3. **ALWAYS LOOK FOR OPPORTUNITIES:** As a high school student, you are probably used to people telling you exactly what to do. You get an assignment rubric for projects, a list of books you should read, and a set number of community service activities you need to do. However, when you want to be an entrepreneur, you need to actively go out and seek opportunities: find chances to learn and meet new people. Branson explained, "Don't

---

21 "Richard". 2020. *Virgin.*

be afraid to get out there and meet like-minded people. Always say yes to opportunities and learn what you need to do to make the most of them as you go along—I've constantly asked for help throughout my life."

4. **FOLLOW YOUR PASSION:** If you are reading this book, you are likely looking to make a difference in your community. Branson stresses how important it is to follow what you truly love: "You'll spend a lot of your life working, but if you're doing something that interests you and you're passionate about, then you'll keep going even when it gets hard (and it will get tough). Think about your talents, what subjects and causes interest you the most, what problems you'd like to solve." If your passion is to create societal change, this will drive you build a social venture you will be proud of. "For [Richard Branson], building a business is all about doing something to be proud of, bringing talented people together and creating something that's going to make a real difference to other people's lives."

5. **DON'T BE AFRAID OF FAILURE:** "I suppose the secret to bouncing back is not only to be unafraid of failures but to use them as motivational and learning tools. There's nothing wrong with making mistakes as long as you don't make the same ones over and over again." Another interesting point he makes is "The brave may not live forever—but the cautious do not live at all!"

6. **READ:** In numerous interviews, Branson mentioned how non-fiction books have greatly influenced him and his outlook on the world.

7. **PROVE DOUBTERS WRONG:** Sometimes when you achieve success, there will be people who will try to doubt you or discredit your work. However, Branson expresses

the best way to combat this is to "not only ignore them, but to prove them wrong in every single way." So what can we learn from Richard Branson? What may be even more important than business knowledge is an entrepreneurial spirit. With no formal business education, Branson has become one of the most respected entrepreneurs in the world.

BILL GATES

At this point, Bill Gates is basically a household name, whether for topping the charts for the worlds richest man for several years, starting Microsoft or launching dozens of philanthropic endeavors through the Bill and Melinda Gates Foundation. He grew up in a wealthy Seattle suburb, and dropped out of Harvard University to start what would eventually become a global tech company with his co-founder Paul Allen. Microsoft started out as a small company that produced software and microprocessors for the early personal computer Altair, went public in 1986 (making Gates the world's youngest billionaire at the time), and by the late 1980s, became the world's largest personal computer software company.[22]

After making a fortune through Microsoft, Gates took part in the Giving Pledge: a commitment by some of the world's

---

22 "Bill & Melinda Gates Foundation". 2020. *Bill & Melinda Gates Foundation*. https://www.gatesfoundation.org/.

most wealthy individuals to donate the majority of their money. The Gates Foundation has embarked on tasks ranging from providing college scholarships to attempting to end the malaria epidemic.[23]

MARK ZUCKERBURG

Mark Zuckerburg, the founder of Facebook, has grown the company from a college dorm into an app that is present on almost every phone in the country. With a valuation in the billions, Facebook is an entrepreneurship venture that is undoubtedly successful, has transformed the social media landscape, and has even been featured in the movie, Social Network. Zuckerburg found his affinity for coding at a young age, and at the age of 12, created his first messaging app for his dad's dental office. While at Harvard, he had a reputation of being a great programmer, and had made two programs: one for helping people enroll in classes with their friends, and one that allowed students to vote on the attractiveness of other students, before eventually launching Facebook out of his dorm. The site started gaining traction, which led to Zuckerburg dropping out sophomore year to move to Palo Alto and work on Facebook in Silicon Valley.

Obviously, the company took off, making Zuckerberg one of the wealthiest men on earth. Like Bill Gates, Zuckerberg has pledged large amounts of money to charity, and is working

---

23 "Microsoft Founded". 2020. *HISTORY.* https://www.history.com/this-day-in-history/microsoft-founded.

on a project to "cure, prevent and manage all diseases in our children's lifetime".[24]

MARK CUBAN

Another Mark who is enacting quite a bit of change in the world. Mark Cuban is an investor on Shark Tank, helping startups with great ideas build their business to the next level, as well as the owner of the Dallas Mavericks. On the show, he always loves to bring up that in order to buy a pair of shoes he wanted, he went around the neighborhood selling trash bags, demonstrating his aptitude for entrepreneurship starting at a very young age. His first business he started out of college was MicroSolutions, a software firm that was eventually sold for 6 million. He saw that it was the perfect time to hop into the online tech industry, and started another compnay that would make him is fortune—AudioNet. Cuban later remaned AudioNet to Broadcast.com and sold to the company to Yahoo for 6 billion.

He later used this money to buy the Dallas Mavericks, revamped it, and eventually transformed the team into one of the best teams in the country, beating the Miami heat in the NBA finals in 2011.[25]

---

24 "Mark Zuckerberg—Facebook, Family & Facts—Biography". 2020. *Biography.Com.*

25 "Andrew Carnegie". 2020. *Biography.* https://www.biography.com/business-figure/andrew-carnegie.

ANDREW CARNEGIE

You have no doubt at least heard of Andrew Carnegie at some point in history class—the 19th century business tycoon who revolutionized the steel industry. He created the Carnegie steel corporation and had steel plants set up all across the country. He had control over not just the production of steel, but the entire supply chain all the way from the mining to the railroads for transporting to producing coal for the furnaces.

When he was 65, he sold his company for 200 million (which is worth a lot more in today's money) to the United States Steel Corporation. Carnegie then dedicated his life to philantropy, building several libraries, making donations, and even establishing the well known Carnegie Mellon University. His philanthropic fund was eventually used to build almost 3,000 libraries, as well as support world peace.

JOHN ROCKEFELLER

Here's another American business tycoon that has this name plastered on buildings and foundations across the country. He founded the Standard Oil Company, which made him one of the wealthiest people in the history of the world. Standard Oil held a monopoly over oil production in the US, and controlled 90% of the country's refineries and pipelines. Some of his business methods, however, were deemed by journalists to be controversial. Since he had such large economies of scale, he was able to produce and sell at a much lower price than competition, driving them out of business. Anti-trust laws in the US eventually allowed the government to break up Standard Oil, but something interesting happened: the smaller companies that Standard Oil was broken into, when combined, became worth more than what Standard Oil was worth. Like Carnegie, he dedicated many of his later years to philanthropy, and donated billions upon billions of dollars to causes such as educational, religious, and scientific causes.[26]

LARRY PAGE AND SERGEY BRIN

Nearly everyone in the world has used Google at one point. However, Larry Page and Sergey Brin, the co-founders and former CEOs of Google's parent company—Alphabet—actually keep a relatively low profile. The pair are among the company's largest shareholders (although they only took a $1 salary while working at Google), and just recently stepped down as co-CEOs. They started the company together in their Stanford dorms in 1995, where Brin was a graduate CS student and Page was considering studying. The company actually was initially named "backrub" until it was changed to Google soon after, a play on the number 1 followed by 100 zeros. After recieving funidng, they both dropped out and worked out of a garage in Menlo Park owned by now CEO of Youtube, Susan Wojkicki. The company rapidly grew and raised funidng, eventually outgrowing the garage and moving to the Googleplex in Mountain View. Google has now moved on from simply creating a search engine to creating a whole slew of different endeavors, ranging from Nest (a smart thermostate) to Google X, what Google calls a "semi-secret research and development facility" working on moonshots—projects equivilent to sending a man to the moon in the 60s.[27]

---

26 "John D. Rockefeller". 2020. *HISTORY.*

27 "Our Stories—Google". 2020. *About.Google.*

ELON MUSK

If you think of a list of traits that define an entrepreneur, changes are, Elon Musk will embody nearly all of them. His commitment to innovation, drive, combined with a touch of quirkiness, have pushed him to revolutionize industries. Musk is most notable for being the CEO and co-founder of Tesla, a company specializing in producing electric cars to, as the company mission states, "transition the world to a sustainable energy future". In addition to spearheading Tesla, he also founded SpaceX, a company that produces advanced rockets and aims to set up a sustainable city on Mars. Elon Musk actually had a hilarious twitter exchange with Mars in February 2019 (make sure to check out his Twitter account). If you think wanting to live on Mars in crazy, he's also working on a project called Neurolink, which is working on connecting the human brain with computers.

Elon Musk was also one of the founding members of PayPal (he joined through a merger, and was fired later due to disagreements with other people in the company). Interestingly, many of the PayPal CEOs and founding members have gone on to create companies that are dominating Silicon Valley, and have even given themselves a name: the PayPal Mafia (I'll elaborate more in the section about Peter Thiel).[28]

PETER THIEL

Peter Thiel is a founder, entrepreneur, and venture capitalist. After getting a philosphy degree and a JD from Stanford, he co-founded PayPal with Max Levchin. Paypal focused

---

28 «Elon Musk | Tesla». 2020. *Tesla.Com.*

on creating a "new world currency" that diverted from the current financial model at the time. Through finding strong hires, Thiel and Levchin found people who would shape the future of Silicon Valley. The initial founders and employees of Paypal went out to start Youtube, LinkedIn, Tesla, and Yelp, among other companies whose combined valuations are worth billions of dollars. These members became the PayPal Mafia, and often turn to each other for either advice or funding or both.

He now runs a venture capital fund, Founder's Fund, and hedge fund, Clarium Capital. He has made many successful investments in unicorns (billion dollar + companies, not flying horses with a horn) such as Facebook, Youtube, and Yelp. Peter Thiel also has a fund that gives 100k, no strings attached, to promising college dropouts.[29]

---

29 "The Paypal Mafia". 2020. *Fortune.*

FINDING AN IDEA

Before you can start a company of any sort, you first need a great idea and a central mission.

With so many issues in the world, how do you narrow it down to one idea to develop and run with? Make sure you choose something that you can truly connect with and can stick to regardless of the obstacles you meet. For many young social entrepreneurs, they find a personal motivation when choosing a topic.

Something that applies not just to social entrepreneurship, but entrepreneurship in general, is to find a problem that needs to be solved. Most successful startups don't begin with the mindset of "Oh, wouldn't it be cool if 'XYZ' existed?" Instead, you need to think along the lines of "Wow! this is an issue that really needs to be solved." That way, you ensure to develop a product or service that is needed by consumers.

Paul Graham from the Y Combinator offers a great summary of this idea:

"When you have an idea for a startup, ask yourself: who wants this right now? Who wants this so much that they'll use it even when it's a crappy version one made by a two-person startup they've never heard of? If you can't answer that, the idea is probably bad."

Three ways to come up with an idea for a social venture that separates it from other companies:

- improve on a concept already developed to make it easier to use
- building a brand around your venture that makes it unique
- come up with a novel idea

DEVELOPING AWARENESS

Coming up with a successful idea typically isn't something you can just sit down for an hour and do, but rather, requires you to be more aware of the world around you. When we are going through our everyday lives, many things simply fly by.

There is a big difference between seeing and *perceiving*. The act of seeing is very physical. Light enters your eyes, and your brain knows the object is there. Perceiving takes another level of awareness—in order to perceive something, you need to actively engage your mind in analyzing and processing the information. Most of the time, when you see something, you don't take time to do this extra step, causing you to overlook problems throughout your day.

This is called **selective attention**, and it has been a pretty prominent psychology experiment. If you want to try it out, look up "selective attention experiment video" (don't read on until you finish because I'm going to spoil the experiment).

Imagine this: you have six people in a room and three of them have white shirts, while the other three have black shirts. These six people are tossing two basketballs around. In the next thirty seconds, you are asked to count the total number of times a person in a white shirt passes a ball. Now, halfway through the experiment, a guy dressed in a giant gorilla costume walks across the back, waves his arms, does a little dance, and walks off the stage. You would notice, right?

Well, when this experiment was being conducted, most people did not realize there was a gorilla at all. This is a perfect example of selective attention, demonstrating how easily we overlook obvious things in our surroundings.

With this in mind, if you are actively *searching* for something—it may be anything ranging from a simple inconvenience to a fundamental issue that is overlooked—chances are, you'll be able to find issues you have never previously considered.

Tomorrow, as you go through your day, think "what could I change to make it better?" If you really want to solidify your ideas, start a little notes section on your phone and jot down every problem you see throughout the day. This increased awareness will go a long way in helping you come up with an idea to create a social venture.

By being more aware of the problems around you, you may come up with an interesting startup idea. Mike Yurosek was a Californian farmer who grew carrots. After months of hard work planting, watering, and tending the crops, all the carrots are taken to the processing plant, where the "ideal" nicely shaped carrots are separated from the less perfect ones. While going through the sorting process, almost seventy percent of the crop would be discarded for aesthetic reasons, which if you put yourself in the position of the farmer, is a huge waste of money and resources. While most farmers couldn't do much to address this issue, Yurosek was determined to find a way to utilize these discards. He bought a potato peeler and reshaped all the misshapen carrots into smaller and more aesthetically pleasing bits; thus, the baby carrot was born.

When he sent these small carrots to a local supermarket, they enthusiastically responded those were perfect, and were the only ones they wanted to purchase. Yurosek's innovative thinking allowed him to solve this age long problem of wasted carrots and created a product that was more convenient for consumers, giving him a place in agricultural history.[30]

BRAINSTORMING TIPS

When you just have a bunch of different ideas floating around in your head, you end up with a very limited list, which often lacks variety. One way to effectively get your ideas down is to use a Google spreadsheet and do a little chart. This way

---

30   "The Invention Of The Baby Carrot". 2020. *Priceonomics.*

is a bit systematic but is great for coming up with things you can do.

In the first column, you put potential target markets. This could be things such as students from underserved areas, people with a certain disease, orphans, the elderly, people without access to clean water, people who care about the environment, and so on.

In the next column, do a bullet list of three to five things that could benefit them. This step is particularly important and should have effort put into it. Make sure to do your research to see what these groups really need, not just what you think they need or what you have heard from others. There have been stories of companies targeting the completely wrong thing with their social venture and end up wasting both time and money. Think about what people really need.

It may help to look at Maslow's Hierarchy of Needs and see what products or services could be created to fulfill these needs. The pyramid has five levels: "physiological," "safety," "belonging and love," "social needs" or "esteem," and "self-actualization." At the base of the pyramid are things everyone needs; once you satisfy one level, you can move up to the next. All five levels are things that social ventures can address.

- Physiological: These are things like sleep, food, shelter, and water—the very basic things that every human needs to survive. Because they are so important to our everyday function, it is essential for these needs to be met, making it a common target for organizations focused on creating social good.

- Safety: This includes both physical and mental well-being. There are people with may be physically safe but are suffering from mental trauma (a prominent example would be soldiers suffering from PTSD despite being in a safe environment at home). Safety includes personal security, emotional security, financial security, and a person's health and well-being.
- Belonging: Once a person has satisfied safety and physiological needs, they look for a sense of belonging through finding acceptance within social groups. This sense of belonging extends to within the family as well.
- Self-esteem: People like to feel respected and valued. This section is better known as a person's "ego."
- Self-actualization: The final part of Maslow's pyramid is achieving a person's maximal potential. After fulfilling each of the lower 4 parts of the pyramid, the person can put time and energy into being the best they could possibly be and achieving their dreams.

Now in column three, start listing things you can do to help address these issues. Keep in mind any limitations you may have (money, time, and people available).

In a fourth column, do a little research on other companies (if they exist) that address or have tried to address the same issue. This will allow you to get a better idea of what things work and what ideas sound good but aren't feasible.

After making these lists, you'll have to spend time deciding which idea is the most feasible and can create the largest impact possible in the most effective way. Here are something things you should keep in mind when making your decision:

- Is this idea scalable?
- How will you get other people interested and involved?
- How much money will you need to raise for this and how will you raise it? (Later in the book is a chapter specifically dedicated to this.)
- Is the idea really needed?

VOLUNTEERING

Since social entrepreneurship ties closely with helping the community, you can definitely get a better idea of what major issues need solving in your community through volunteering.

Corrine Clinch, CEO of Rorus and Forbes 30 Under 30 social entrepreneur, got her inspiration from a volunteer trip in Africa. After studying biomedical and civil engineering in college, Corrine found a way to put this knowledge into use in international aid. While on this trip, she realized the extent of the water crisis around the world, driving her to create Rorus. Rorus is an easy and portable water filtration system that utilizes nanotechnology to filter out harmful substances in water and can provide a family with clean water for up to half a year.

However, the idea is only the seed of your venture. What separates a successful organization from one that fails is the execution of the idea. Once you finish developing your idea, do a quick Google search to see if you can find anything else similar online. If you do see another organization doing the same thing, consider a couple things: are there different areas of impact? Do you think you could do a better job? Is the existing organization large and well-funded, or is it a smaller startup?

If someone else is doing what you had in mind, it doesn't automatically mean you need to switch ideas. Quite a while ago, there was a company called ConnectU, which was basically a social networking site focused on connecting people with their peers. They were actually founded before Facebook and accused Zuckerberg of stealing their idea. However, despite the two of them building a company for the same thing, Facebook is successful, while ConnectU has faded from existence. Why? Because in addition to having a good idea, there needs to be good execution to bring that idea into reality.

LOOK TO OTHER SOCIAL VENTURES FOR INSPIRATION

There are many resources for learning more about people who have launched successful (and unsuccessful) social ventures around the world. A great site you can check out is http://inspiringsocialentrepreneurs.com/, where they have weekly podcasts of an interview with a successful social entrepreneur. In a previous chapter, I introduced some interesting social ventures from which you can draw inspiration and learn, so if you would like, feel free to flip back and take another look at them (Flora, Oxy2, Toms, and more!) A quick Google search can help you find even more existing startups within the field you want to enter.

TAKEAWAYS:
Creating a startup is about solving a problem. In order to be successful, you need to do something called "need finding"—discovering a problem your audience has and solving it. Start-up ideas stem from anything ranging from an epiphany you have while volunteering to an idea that emerges after hours of brainstorming. Just make sure to be actively aware of everything that comes up in your life and keep an eye out for hidden problems that need solving!

MAKING A TEAM

———

In most situations, one person can't do it all. This is definitely the case for many businesses, especially startups. If you take a look at successful companies (of any type really, not just social entrepreneurships), you will find almost all of them have at least one thing in common—they started with a team. If you take a look at statistics regarding why startups fail, not having the right team is high up on the list, with almost a quarter of companies listing it as the main reason their organization went under.[31]

Blueprints for Pangaea is a student run organization that collects unused medical supplies that are no longer wanted from hospitals and redistributing them to places in need of them. This idea was started at Michigan State University by Ben Rathi. In just a year, the organization has greatly expanded, and is now present at multiple schools. However, in an interview with the founder, he noted that one of the biggest things he would change if he had the opportunity

———

31 "How To Build A Team That Won't Sink Your Startup". 2020. *Neil Patel.*

to do it all over again would be to find a group of people passionate about the cause to work with him on it earlier.

Clarence Tan, the CEO of Boddle, an integrated educational gaming system, tells a similar story. While he founded this technology-based company, he did not personally have a strong background in computer science and product design, so instead, found someone else to take care of this side of the company while he managed more of the business matters.

This doesn't mean you can't be the sole President or CEO of a company—you just need to find a group of people with just the right skills and the passion to grow your venture with you. So how do you find the perfect team that will not only work in the startup stages of an organization, but also further down the road? Come up with a general idea of what aspects of your business you would like to focus on; these are things like marketing, product research, web design, finance, and so on.

You need to begin with seeing what you can personally accomplish, and what skills will best complement yours. Great self-awareness is incredibly important in finding and ideal group and making sure that your group functions cohesively toward achieving a common goal. If you like to do the business side of things but want to create a tech related startup, find someone who loves to code and build things. In addition to having skillsets that match up, it is equally important to find people you can connect to and see yourself working with in the long run. One of the worst mistakes you could make is finding someone who has the skills you are looking for, but has a personality that just doesn't click with yours, leaving the two of you at constant odds when debating what direction you want to take the company.

Now, when I say find teammates that can complement your skillset, it is important to avoid homogeneity. If you have a group of people who are too similar, you may end up with people who think and act the same way. This typically ends up causing a problem with developing new ideas. When everyone thinks the same way, it also opens the door to people all missing the same problems that arise.

What's more, if the CEO doesn't own the majority of shares, he or she can be removed from the company. As seen in the news, as well as pop culture (remember the 2008 *Iron Man* movie where the villain tried to remove Stark from his company?) this happens in real life.

If you are funding your company by giving away shares and end up with others owning more than fifty percent of your startup, you leave yourself vulnerable to being fired. The founder/CEO can be fired through a vote by the board, and if people with more than half the shares vote to fire you, you're gone.

There are stories of this happening to co-founders as well. Michael Slavin did this with his co-founder, who he found to be slacking off. While funding their company, they gave away six and a half percent to investors, leaving them each with forty-six and three-quarters percent of the company each. While neither of them held the majority, Slavin convinced the investors to give him their voting rights. Now, with fifty-three percent of the voting rights, Slavin was able to force his partner to either buy out (sell the rest of his shares) or be fired from the company.

A more high-profile example of a founder getting kicked out of their own company is Steve Jobs. A couple years into the business, the board of directors decided they did not like Steve Jobs' personality and way of handling things and decided to fire him. Interestingly, the stock prices dropped after Jobs left, and when he later rejoined the company, the value went back up.

While this happened, it isn't something that occurs too often. You could put not being able to fire the CEO in a contract, however, many times, the CEO looks out for the interests of the company, and if it is more beneficial for someone else to take his or her place, then they will usually willingly step down.

Throughout these stories, you begin to see a bit of a pattern. Often it is more advantageous to start an organization solo, and then recruit other members to help ensure you have maximum control over your startup.

When you are starting up, it is good to keep the founding team small to allow for closer communication. Positions such as design manager, finances, marketing, and organization are all helpful for a startup. As the organization grows, start recruiting more people who care about and are willing to put time and effort into the cause.

Blueprints for Pangea founder shares how he organized his student-run organization to make it as effective as possible.

In an interview, he noted, "When we first started our chapter it was just a team of 4 of us and we had a mini- eboard of 5-6 other people, but we never had regular meetings and we didn't really have many team members. Now, we have a large eboard and a large committee, both who are very passionate about our cause and give us more people to make a larger impact on our community. This has been a very successful year, but it has also been a year for a lot of growth. We know where we need to improve upon for next year, and I am looking forward to all of the incredible things we do in the future."

BUILDING TEAM CULTURE

Once you have successfully created a team, you need to ensure that the team is actively engaged and motivated. Have you ever been part of a group project where you had to keep bugging your other groupmates to finish their part, and after giving up on making them do their part, ending up doing it for them? That is probably one of the worst situations you would want to find you and your team in.

Research has shown that successful teams are able to effectively communicate in a judgement-free environment. This doesn't mean that any criticism should be avoided—everyone should feel comfortable sharing their opinion.

A group of MIT researchers conducted a study to determine what affects the efficiency of groups. To do this, they found groups of people from all walks of life: MBA students, engineers, CEOs, and a group of kindergarteners. Each group was given the same task of building the tallest tower possible using a limited supply of spaghetti and marshmallows.

Most people expected the MBA students or the engineers to win. After all, don't they have the most experience working together and solving difficult problems? However, to everyone's surprise, the groups of kindergarteners consistently out-performed some of the professional students. Upon further analysis of the groups' behaviors during the task, the researchers found a couple of differentiating factors between the kindergarteners and the adults.

While building the structure, the kids were able to communicate in an open and unrestrained way. As opposed to the adults who tried to instill a form of structure, and subtly jockeyed for leadership within the groups, the kindergarteners simply focused on creatively working together toward their goal.

Something else that has been shown to drastically improve productivity is to create a team culture. Instead of having your startup be another task one of your team members needs to do, make working on the project together fun. While staying focused on your project is good, be sure to occasionally plan some team bonding activities (this can be as simple as grabbing lunch together or going on a hiking trip) to create stronger relationships among team members.

When having team discussions, make sure you don't single anyone out for mistakes. Doing so may create toxicity within your team, and a feeling of resentment toward you. Instead, either discuss the issue as a whole or talk to that person individually.

COMMUNICATION

How you want to set up communication within your team largely depends on how exactly your team is organized. Do you see each other in person often? Do you all have busy schedules, or can you devote a lot of time to this project? Are there time zone differences? How big is your team? These are all things you should consider.

CHATROOMS

With almost everyone having easy access to a phone or the Internet, a great thing to start with is a group chat with all members of the leadership team. This can be done on platforms such as Facebook Messenger, or on specialized workplace team communication platforms such as Facebook Workchat, Slack, or Groupme. They all have their own unique qualities: some are good for lots of subgroups, allow you to create a hierarchy, make announcements, assign work, and so on, so take some time to look at all of them and see which ones fit your needs best.

VIDEO CONFERENCES

Chatrooms are very convenient for your team to communicate; however, there are always situations requiring many of your team to be on at the same time so decisions can be made and any questions or confusion can be quickly resolved. You get to have more productive face to face interaction without needing to waste time traveling.

I have found that Zoom is one of the best platforms for hosting video conferences. You can set up the meeting through the app and send out a meeting link and a calendar invite to all participants, who can join once the meeting starts either via a video call or through a phone call. One of the best features is the ability to record the meeting and send it out as a YouTube link to any team members who didn't make the meeting, or if anyone wants to review any details later. Other popular platforms include Skype, Slack, and Google Hangouts, so feel free to explore and see which one best fits the needs of your venture. To help ensure your meeting is organized and concise, here are some pointers to follow:

HOW TO HOLD A SUCCESSFUL VIDEO CONFERENCE

- Set an agenda. One of the worst things you can do is show up to the meeting not entirely sure about what to talk about or go through the meeting and realize afterwards that there were key issues that you forgot to discuss. Before each meeting, create a short outline of everything you would like to discuss, and if needed, assign people topics that they should study to make sure the meeting is as productive as possible. Always leave time for questions and additional comments throughout the call. Sometimes when you are the primary speaker, your team members may be hesitant to jump in, so make these opportunities clear.
- Consider creating visuals. Along with your agenda, throw together a quick PowerPoint you can run through during the meeting to keep everyone on task, and make sure nothing gets left out. Visuals also help make the meeting a bit more engaging, while graphs and charts can help you express your ideas much more clearly.

- Be concise. Don't waste everyone's time by rambling about insignificant ideas, or using too much of the group's time to just address one person or a small part of your team. Staying relevant and on-topic keeps members from muting the call and zoning out. Instead, put some thought into who to include and what to discuss in each call. One large call with everyone may seem like the fastest way to get points across, but these may become chaotic and prevent some people from sharing their opinions. Instead, create separate group calls to discuss different topics to promote more meaningful discussion.

TAKEAWAYS:

Creating a great team is essential to a startup's success. There are several factors you should consider when finding people to join your team and creating a great team environment!

- Find people who complement your skills and add to the company culture
- Choose a platform to communicate over
- Maintain regular communication and check-ins

MAKING A PLAN

———

There are assignments in school you can pull together the night before, or a presentation that you can improvise on the spot, but when it comes to starting a company, it is always good to have a plan. While there is debate about whether a business plan is necessary to success, as a student, you definitely do not have the experience to just "wing it" in the business world. The Panel of Entrepreneurial Dynamics has an ongoing study where over 800 founders are reviewed, and has found people with business plans are two and a half times more likely to get started with a business.[32]

When it comes to a business plan, each business will have a unique path, which they should follow. However, things essential to the business's success, should be included in each one.

———

32 Henricks, Mark. 2020. "Do You Really Need A Business Plan?". *Entrepreneur.*

BUSINESS IDEA

This is the first thing you must figure out. Once you come up with an idea you are satisfied with, keep in mind that it does not need to be set in stone. As you do market research, feel free to adjust this idea as needed to best suit your cause.

Things to think about or include:

- Why you decided to start this organization
- What the organization will accomplish
- How your startup will get to this end goal
- How does your idea differ from what is already established?
- Why are you qualified to launch this startup, and how does it align with your talent and skillset?
- Money. Where will you get the capital? You can't do much without money.

MARKET RESEARCH

A big mistake new entrepreneurs make is not aligning their product with what the customers want when starting out, resulting in large amounts of wasted capital.

When you first begin, you are going to think you have a wonderful idea (which it probably is), but what is even more important is how well the community will respond to it. To find out, you need to do some market research. This research advice can be used beyond researching for your startup. The tips here can help you with typical school projects and assignments.

You should have several goals to aim for when conducting market research. These will help you get a clearer idea about what you want to do and how to best accomplish it.

COMPETITION

Initially, you should invest time studying the marketplace to see if there are any competitors trying to do the same thing as you. What have they done that worked well? If they are not doing so well, what mistakes did they make?

Using the competition as an example will save you a great deal of time and money and allow you to better refine your venture's direction. Try to find at least three to four other companies doing something similar. If your idea is unique, instead of finding people doing the same thing as you, try to find someone who is tackling the same goal, even if it is through different means. If you cannot find anyone addressing the same issue, you might want to take a step back and consider why. Many companies and NGOs have plenty of resources, and if they aren't trying to solve a glaring problem, there may be a reason behind that.

UNDERSTANDING THE PROBLEM

Now that you have an idea, it may be tempted to jump in headfirst. You will probably have a huge burst of excitement and motivation when just starting out, but you need to make sure that you know what you are doing.

What some people don't see is you need to not just know about but *understand* the issue at hand. Countless stories abound of excited entrepreneurs diving into an idea and then realizing a major flaw to their plan.

Recently, a team at Carnegie Mellon decided to embark on a project to help the issue of premature births in Africa. Every day, hundreds of mothers and babies die from premature or unsuccessful deliveries, so of course, this was a worthy cause. They spent months fundraising, planning, and designing a low-cost incubator for premature babies. When the team finally arrived in the town, they realized they had completely missed the mark.

There were incubators piled in hospital rooms. What was the real problem? Getting the women medical care in time.

If the team had done more extensive research into the specific conditions of the people their product is targeted toward, they would have saved enormous amounts of time and money.

Before investing in your project, make certain you have a thorough understanding of why the service you provide is needed. Are there any other companies that have tried to do the same thing? If so, see if they have been successful. Take time to analyze what makes companies in your field fail or succeed.

A big mistake social entrepreneurs make is not focusing on whether their product or service is something people want and are willing to pay for. The profit margins need to be large enough so the company has enough funding to remain sustainable. You must look at your costs of production to make sure they are reasonable, and that your idea will be sustainable in the long run.

TALK TO PEOPLE

A great way to learn more about a specific field is to talk to people experienced in that field. Set up a meeting with a teacher or professor who is knowledgeable about whatever issue you want to tackle. Visit and talk with the people or groups you are trying to help. No matter what the idea is, always get to know your issue inside and out. When talking to Clarence, he emphasized there is a huge difference between having read everything about a problem and seeing it first hand. This sentiment resounds through many different interviews.

PICK A NAME

When naming your venture, make certain it is memorable. When you think of successful social entrepreneurship companies, which ones come to mind? Probably ones that have interesting, simple, memorable, and relevant names—Google, Facebook, Uber, Lyft, YouTube, etc. The name you settle on will end up becoming your brand, so choose well!

Richard Branson, a billionaire serial entrepreneur, is the founder of the Virgin Group. There is no doubt this name is eye-catching for obvious reasons—so why did he choose it?

When he was first starting his company in his early twenties, he was having drinks with a group of friends about a name for his record store: "A bunch of ideas were bounced around, then, as we were all new to business, someone suggested Virgin. It smacked of new and fresh and at the time the word was still slightly risqué, so, thinking it would be an attention-grabber, we went with it."

When coming up with names, try to avoid acronyms. While there are successful companies with acronym names (think BBC and IBM), it is hard to remember exactly what the company does from a few letters.

A smarter approach would be to do a word mash-up of things your startup will try to accomplish.

Also, make sure you can get an available URL of the startup name. This is important for building a website later.

MAKE A WEBSITE
Whether or not you have coding or web design experience, making a simple website isn't too difficult to do. Sites such as Weebly or Wix are very user friendly and have a low monthly fee, but there are many others. The free versions you can use generally won't let you use your own domain name (which you can buy through GoDaddy or Google Domains for under $20 a year). If you don't feel up to this challenge, find someone to join the team who has some experience in website creation or design or hire a freelance website designer.

The number one thing to keep in mind when designing the website is the question: 'What should the visitor take away after visiting the site?' You need to really emphasize your mission and how someone can contribute.

Here is a list of things you should make sure to include:

- A clear mission statement
- Information about your startup and your goals
- Any products or services you are selling
- A team page to introduce the core members of your team
- Clear messages you want to convey

SETTING GOALS

"If you don't know where you are going, you might not get there."
—YOGI BERRA

Think about what change you want to enact, and to what degree; this will create your vision for what you want your social venture to achieve. However, making a good goal isn't just as simple as coming up with something you want to achieve. When you format a goal in the right way, it helps outline key steps and milestones that you will pass in order to achieve it. In other words, it'll make sure your work is cut out for you. When setting your goals, here are some things you should keep in mind:

MAKE GOALS QUANTITATIVE

"Making [group of people XYZ] happy" may sound like a great thing to accomplish, but it is almost always better for goals to be measurable. There are multiple quantitative measures you can look at: sales, donations, customer satisfaction rating, and more. Hitting these goals will give you a clear indication of if you are on track for success.

HAVE BOTH SHORT-TERM AND LONG-TERM MILESTONES

Sometimes when you have a goal that is too large and is set too far in the future, you will burn out before reaching it. It is great to have an overarching goal, but you need to make sure you break it down into manageable chunks. For example, a more long-term goal for a company that matches clothing sales with a free item of clothing for someone in poverty could be to donate 100,000 shirts in 2020. To break it down a bit, first see how many shirts you will need to sell per month, if you expect your sales to grow over the course of the year or stay relatively stable, how many ads you want to run, how many website visits you want, how many followers you have on social media, and so on. When you have a more precise outline of what you want to accomplish per month, you have a much more reasonable list of milestones you need to hit in order to reach your overarching goal of 100,000 shirts donated.

KEEP YOURSELF ACCOUNTABLE

Find someone or something to keep yourself accountable for reaching your goals. While you may be excited early on, it is easy to get a little bored a couple months in and having a friend or partner to help remind you about and keep you accountable for your goals is essential.

OKR

An interesting goal setting system used by many Fortune 500 companies and successful CEOs is known as OKR, or Objective Key Results. It became more well-known after being a core method of goal setting used at tech giant,

Google. This system helps you and your team shoot for one unified goal while knowing what indicators of success you should be watching. There are two parts: the objective and the key results.

You should come up with three to five objectives that are ambitious yet realistic, specific, and actionable. An example of this would be something like "improving customer satisfaction by the end of the year." These objectives should ideally be ambitious enough that you aren't hitting every single target. At Google, the guideline is the goals should be met about seven out of ten times.

Key results are measurable milestones and can indicate progress toward the objective. For the customer satisfaction example, the key results would be items such as "have fifty five-star reviews" and "have average review score go up by one point."[33]

Creating an OKR ensures that each member of your team knows what your social venture needs to accomplish within a specific timeframe and takes measures to hit these goals. This adds accountability within you group as well, ultimately leading a higher likelihood of meeting your goals.

You can find a nice sample OKR template online.

---

33   "Okrs". 2020. *Medium.*

ADJUSTING YOUR PLANS

——

Since communities are constantly changing, you need to be able to keep an open mind and change your original idea, if needed. When your idea doesn't seem to be working, **do not waste too much time trying to convince yourself that this original idea is perfect.**

A psychological principle affecting humans is we value consistency, which means we will inherently have a desire to align our actions with our inner perspectives and values. Because of this, when we conduct an act, we realign what we think to match this action. If our beliefs and our actions don't match, we experience a phenomenon called *cognitive dissonance*, which may lead to us adjusting our beliefs to suit the action.

For example, if you decide to embark on a specific advertising campaign, you may begin to convince yourself it was a good idea regardless of the results. Consumers who have purchased a specific brand in the past, whether it is something as cheap as fast food or as pricey as a car, will likely stick to that brand, even if it happens to decrease in quality or increase in price. After a college student goes through the difficult process of rushing a fraternity or sorority, they are much more likely to remain an active part of the organization, partially as a result of thinking they need to remain consistent to and create value out of their efforts to join.

This need for consistency can be quite dangerous for a startup. However, once you are aware of this concept, keep it in mind when making decisions; are you making a decision based on the current situation? Or are you just keeping in line with previous decisions you have made?

When starting a company, you need to be flexible and know when to adjust your idea to be a better fit for the group you are trying to benefit.

Many of you have seen the picture comparing classrooms from a hundred years ago to classrooms today. Shockingly, aside from the black and white photography, there has been virtually no change in our educational systems. How is it possible in a society with rapidly evolving technology, this technological innovation has not been applied to classrooms? College student Clarence Tan realized this issue and decided to create video games to help students learn educational concepts. Clarence and his team started an educational video game company, however doing this didn't differentiate them from the countless apps out there that do essentially the same thing—helping kids with reading comprehension, math, science, or history. None of these integrated technology into a comprehensive system to help students learn. This realization drove Clarence to scrap his old idea and start a new company: Boddle.

Instead of creating, let's say a math game, Boddle works with teachers to integrate technological learning into the classroom. The cute Boddle head characters will follow the students through everything from learning new topics to homework to assessments. Essentially, the curriculum can be adapted into a game—a much more engaging learning method that caters toward children's short attention spans. This startup drew lots of support ranging from individual teachers to being sponsored by national governments.

Clarence immediately knew he steered the company in the right direction, once he saw the eyes of elementary schoolers light up as they were using the software. This alteration in the business model allowed Boddle to become not just a company that cultivates a love of learning, but also gives teachers ease and flexibility.

What initially seemed liked a great idea can always be improved on, which is why it is so essential to keep this open mindset when running your business.

PRODUCT/IDEA TESTING AND RESEARCH

Once you have your idea and decide to get started, you need to make sure that what you are offering aligns closely with what consumers want. Reviews, emails, changes in sales, and so on, should tip you off that your idea and consumers don't "click." Before you dive in, test your idea with a small group of people to make sure the idea is as good as you thought it would be.

- Talk to the people you know (friends, family, teachers, classmates) to get their opinion on your idea.
- Share a short survey with anyone and everyone you can get ahold of. While it may be easier to just try to reach your target market, there may be people interested in your idea you haven't even thought of.
- Interview people in the target audience you have defined using your survey to see how you can optimize your good or service to fit their needs.

Things to ask:

- Do they experience "problem you are trying to solve"?
- Is there any way they are already tackling this problem?
- How much would they pay for your good or service?
- Do they have any suggestions for you to improve your idea?
- Who would they think is the target audience for this product?

TAKEAWAYS

- After coming up with an idea, it's time to lay out what you need to do in the short and long run in order to achieve your goals (OKRs are a great goal setting technique).
- Do research on both the problem and other companies who are working on solving the same problem.
- Be flexible and willing to change the direction of your company if things aren't working out.

GETTING FUNDING

———

Have you ever watched an episode of *Shark Tank* and heard the words "seed funding," "series A funding," "venture capital," "equity funding," and "angel investors?" In this chapter, you'll learn all the jargon associated with business funding, so you can see which one is the best for your venture.

There is almost no value to the greatest of ideas unless they can be implemented, and in our modern society, what is the one thing you will always need to get nearly anything done in a business? Money. No matter what cause you decide to focus on and what business model you choose to pursue, there will always be a need for money to get your idea up and running.

Now, several ways you can go about getting this initial capital is from community support to private investors to grants. Depending on the goals of the venture, different sources of funding may make more sense for different startups. However, the terminology for these funding types are important to know if you want to come off as confident and knowledgeable.

TYPES OF FUNDING FOR STARTUPS

- You! AKA bootstrapping: Unless you have a lot of money to invest in your startup, this is the small amount of money that you need to put in early on (typically out of pocket) in order to get your idea going. Any money earned early on should be invested back into the business. This gives you total control over your business, however, completely funding your company on your own may make you miss out on mentorship and connections you may gain from investors (who want you to succeed so that they can earn money).

- When you are first getting started, it is a good idea to look for some "mini-grants" to get the startup off the ground. These are especially good when you are not entirely sure about what direction you want to take the startup in. Let's say you want to create a piece of technology that will help improve medical care in a third world country but haven't made enough sales to convince an investor to put money into your company—one of these mini grants would be a great place to start. There are numerous organizations that give out these grants (usually under $1000) depending on the cause they focus. In an interview with Clarence Tan, he indicated he was able to receive several small grants from organizations such as Peacefirst. Often organizations focusing on helping students make an impact on the world, and these are a great place to get funding.

- Many universities have opportunities for students to obtain funding from the school for their startup. This is usually either in the form of a grant, participating in an accelerator, or an entrepreneurship competition/ challenge. If your school doesn't offer anything like that, sometimes other local schools have opportunities open to students beyond just those who attend their school.

- Crowdfunding: This basically means raising money from other people. I'm sure you have heard of numerous online crowdfunding platforms such as GoFundMe or Indiegogo. There is always no harm in setting up a crowdfunding page and seeing if you can get people to donate. From my experience seeing different crowdfunding campaigns, what really makes or breaks the campaign is its ability to gain momentum and be shared among groups of people. For many crowdfunding platforms, you are able can offer small perks or rewards for donating a specific amount.

    - Individually request people to donate—although posting on social media or sending out a big BCC'd email may save time, individually asking people to contribute to your campaign will maximize the response rate. Additionally, it is definitely beneficial to meet people either in person or talk over a phone call to explain what your social venture does.
    - Make a promotional video to help engage potential donors.
    - Hold an event to launch the campaign. This could be a neighborhood party or an event in a rented facility. Make sure you have lots of things for people to take pictures of and share on social media.
    - Try to get media attention. You can reach out to local news sources (you can find these through a quick google search). Send a couple of them a little bit of information about your startup and see if anyone would be willing to write a story about it. You could also search for individual writers who have done stories on similar things before.

EQUITY INVESTORS

Usually with equity funding, there are several rounds where money can be raised. For a typical student led social venture, extremely large amounts of funding aren't needed, so I'll just do a brief overview of the funding rounds.

- Seed funding: At this point, your startup is just a seed that will (hopefully) grow into something great! This is the first round of funding that is needed to get the company started and will usually be a smaller number—for a student run, new organization with a great idea this will be likely be under half a million dollars.
- Series A: Here, you need more than a proof of concept. You need to show the investors that there is a market for your product/idea. There is something called the "Series A crunch," where startups that were able to raise early stage seed funding are unable to obtain more funding and thus, end up fading out.
- Series B: You have your product down and a customer base. Now you want to expand! Series B funding is what you need to grow your business.
- Series C: If you make it here, this means your business is doing very well. Series C is mostly for people who want to seriously grow their company and expand, perhaps even internationally.
- Series D & E: This is if your company is failing and you need more capital, or the business is doing so well you can't keep up. The large majority of companies don't make it here, and it is mostly for those who are about to go public.

ANGEL INVESTORS

Ah... the Catch22 of startups. It is hard to get funding without something to prove that your idea works. However, in order to prove that your company will be successful, you need funding. This is where some people turn to what are called Angel Investors. Essentially, these people, often rich, use their own money to invest in startups as opposed to having someone else manage their funds for them. These Angel Investors typically offer less money than venture capitalists, but it is a good place to get started. Additionally, they often are current (or ex) entrepreneurs that may have knowledge in the area you are working. This is the type that you see on *Shark Tank*: "Good morning ... blah blah blah ... I'm seeking $300,000 in return for thirty percent of my company." In this case, you not only want to use them as a source of funding, but also as an area of expertise as well. They may be someone who is knowledgeable or accomplished in the area that you are trying to go into.

However, in order to find these angel investors, you need to do a bit of research. There are several good websites that help pair entrepreneurs with angel investors:

- Angel Capital Association
- Gust
- The BC Angel Forum

If you are coming up with new technology which has not been tested or proven, angel investors are often the best way to go. Yuja Chang was able to launch his company by finding an angel investor who sympathized with the cause he was targeting—helping the blind navigate in their daily lives.

Especially as a student, you may have trouble finding investors that will have faith in a student run company. Thus, it is important to research and convince someone who cares about your cause to invest. Since money from angel investors comes from an individual, it is much easier to emotionally appeal to them as opposed to a venture capital firm.

VENTURE CAPITAL

Now, if you are a student starting out with a small startup idea and that the primary purpose of your social venture isn't to maximize profit, venture capital likely isn't your best option. However, this information may come in to use later in your journey as an entrepreneur. Venture capital firms typically have professional investors who search for startups with long-term potential and invest in amounts typically exceeding a million dollars. These funds often have a very large fund and invest money for both equity and seats on a startup's board. This could potentially create a situation where the investors make up a larger portion of the company than the founder/CEO, giving them the power to fire the founder. Venture capitalists are well connected and can really help you grow your business to the next level; however, they aren't an option for most small startups. Yet, as always, there are extraordinary people who can make an exception (this can also be you!).

I've taken a class at Stanford taught by a well-known venture capitalist, and one thing he really emphasized was pitching a big market—basically showing the company has the potential to become the next billion dollar idea. This is a result of the structure of venture capital funds and how they make money (it's interesting, if you want to look more into it). Keep in mind that while social ventures are created for social impact, it doesn't have to be a nonprofit.

Jia Jun Shaw is the fifteen-year-old founder of the Rejuvenate Project, where he and some friends helped low income elderly individuals by chatting with them and helping them do some household chores. It was your typical small community service group. However, as a dare from a friend, he began to cold call large firms around the world to ask for financial backing. That dare was one of the biggest turning points in his charity. Despite facing rejection after rejection, Shaw focused on the potential impact he could be making and eventually earned the support of Cambridge Associates and Ben & Jerry's as well as three governmental organizations in Singapore. Perhaps most significantly, he received financial backing from Impact Venture Solutions, a major international venture capital firm. Is this the norm? No. But Shaw's story shows that with enough grit and perseverance (not to sound cliché), anything is possible.

STRATEGIC PARTNERS

While many angel investors and venture capitalists aim to do whatever they need to do to increase their return on investment, strategic partners are often people or companies that have a strategic interest in your business. Perhaps you are developing something their company can use in the future. While they typically are willing to settle for a high valuation, they want equity in addition to something else. This is what separates them from the other types of investors. This would be things such as licensing agreements, distribution contracts, or the opportunity to buy the company in the future.

Strategic investors are great, if you are looking for something beyond just cash for your business. You need to understand one hundred percent what they are looking to get out of your startup, and then decide as to whether this is a reasonable tradeoff for the extra funding. An important thing to keep in mind when finding a strategic partner is not being forced into a corner and agree to something that would end up hindering your venture's goals.

LOANS

Unlike the other options above, a you need to pay back the money you get from taking out a loan with the amount borrowed plus interest, so it can place a bit of pressure on the company. However, the good thing about loans is you don't need to give up equity in your venture.

Texan billionaire Mark Cuban warns not to not give up too much equity. He said the further you can go with a business, the better off you are because you are not weighed down by the need to impress investors. You still need to maintain the ability to focus on the target audience and continue to provide products or services that will create a positive community impact.

Now of course, the goal of a social entrepreneurship company that makes it differ from a nonprofit is it needs to be financially self-sustaining and not rely on a constant stream of grants and donors. Since every startup is unique and is started with a different set of circumstances, you need to find the source of funding that will work best and make the most sense for you.

PUBLIC SPEAKING

Ok so now you have an idea and a team. Now, you need to get community support for your organization. Chances are, you will probably be asked to give presentations or talks, or at the very least be able to give an overview of your venture over the phone or at a meeting. Even if you aren't forced into position where you need to public speak, being able to do so will give you many advantages in terms of the opportunities you will be able to access and potential investments you may achieve.

HOW TO BECOME A BETTER PUBLIC SPEAKER

America's number one fear is not spiders or car crashes or even death—it is the fear of public speaking. In fact, many students are not comfortable with public speaking simply because they haven't gotten enough practice. While public speaking seems difficult, it is definitely something that can be improved. To really understand where this nervousness caused by public speaking comes from, let's look as the very basic physiological basis of this anxiety. When confronted with something we perceive as frightening, which in this case is public speaking, our body kicks into a fight or flight response that leads to hyperarousal—all our senses are heightened, and blood is directed to our vital organs, the brain and the heart.

A trick some people use to reduce hyperventilation before a presentation is breathing from a paper bag (or your hands) for a few seconds. A momentary increase in carbon dioxide triggers a couple of physiological mechanisms which lower both heart and breathing rates.

There are several different theories regarding public speaking and the fear of public speaking. In most of these, the causes stem from the things below.

WHAT CAUSES A FEAR OF PUBLIC SPEAKING?

Negative Thoughts

One of the worst things you can do is try to convince yourself you are horrible at public speaking and are going to fail before even getting the chance to present. Not only does this not benefit you in any way, but also it may hurt your performance. Being prepared for a presentation is good. Worrying about it only causes anxiety and will make you more nervous when you are on the spot.

According to Neuropsychologist Theo Tsaousides, there are two different ways for you to perceive your public speaking event—a performance orientation and a community orientation. Which attitude you take on may greatly influence your mindset during the presentation, and thus, the quality of it.

Performance orientation is the idea that you are trying to prove to the judges that you are a good presenter. You think public speaking requires a great deal of specific skills, and if you use these techniques, you will be successful. In other words, you are trying to impress the audience. You are worried too much about what you're wearing, whether you know every little detail about the topic, and so on. This is commonly noted as the mindset that leads to overwhelming public speaking anxiety and a difficulty in getting the message across to your audience.

Instead of taking on the performance orientation, a perspective which will help you successfully convey your message to the audience is the community orientation. A community orientation focuses more on your ideas and makes certain whoever is listening to your presentation walks away with a solid sense of what you talked about. This orientation will allow you to deliver your information in a more relaxed and likely more understandable manner. Imagine your presentation is just another conversation with a group of friends, and you are trying to explain a concept to them.

When you think you are being evaluated, you will be a lot more anxious than if you think they are just trying to learn from you. Changing your mindset here can make a big difference in how good your speech or presentation is.

Tell a Story

Begin every presentation with a story. Stories have been used by societies dating all the way back to paintings scribbled on caves thousands of years ago. What about stories makes them so special? Stories allow a speaker to immerse others in their own experiences, creating a personal connection in the community. It allows us to understand beyond superficial facts. Stories invoke curiosity, captivating the audience, making them want to learn more. It is not a coincidence that ancient Greek society was built around tales of Zeus' power and fury, or that even in the modern day, people flood theaters to experience the life of another person for just an hour or two, or how companies structure their advertisements based on a story.

But Why? What about our brains makes us immerse ourselves in and connect with these stories? Our brains have "mirror neurons" that allow us to *feel* when hearing a story, allowing it to invoke an emotional response by causing large increases in oxytocin, building a strong, mental connection.

Geoffrey Berwind, a professional business consultant, shares with *Forbes* why story telling is such a powerful technique. He says in order to better understand the influence of storytelling, we have to rewind to when we were kids.

Our affinity for stories has a biological basis as well. Some researchers in Spain did a study on how our brain reacts to hearing stories. They found when someone is listening to a story, not only is the language processing region of the brain activated, as expected, but the parts of the brain that would be activated if the audience was actually experiencing the story lit up. What may be even more intriguing is something called neural coupling occurs: the same parts of the speaker's brain and the listeners brain lit up.

You don't have to limit your presentations to just having a story within them; you can also structure presentations in the form of a story to keep the audience engaged. Have a beginning where you introduce the problem, how dissatisfied you are with the status quo, and throw in a story of someone affected by the issue. In the middle, introduce the conflict by contrasting "what is" with "what could be," drawing attention from the audience. Finally, you can conclude with the end of the journey—what you envision the end goal to be after the implementation of whatever idea you are proposing.

This means by telling a story in your presentation, you actively engage your listeners, allowing them to both follow along better, and become more interested in your idea. https://www.forbes.com/sites/rodgerdeanduncan/2014/01/04/tap-the-power-of-storytelling/#76838925614a

Lack of Practice

While it is important to adopt a positive mindset when you are speaking, it is equally important to keep in mind that you should never just "wing" an important presentation, no matter how great you think you are at public speaking. If you do that, you will likely forget important points which will reduce the validity of your presentation. Instead, practice your presentation a few times and make a short, bulleted list either on paper or in your head of all the points you are going to cover.

You want to have better speaking skills

Everyone speaks differently, and these differences can either make your performance more effective or less effective. So what can you do to make sure you don't come off as the awkward person who mumbles their way through a presentation, or rushes through it at the speed of light allowing no one to understand what they are saying?

- Find a Toastmasters session near you.
- Body language matters: make sure you maintain good posture and come off as confident. Use arm gestures to better engage the audience; however, don't flail your arms around. A general rule of thumb is to keep your arms in an imaginary box which spans the upper half of your torso.
- Watch recordings of your speeches. This is one of the best ways to improve on the small things you dislike with your speech. If you think you don't speak clearly enough, try to pinpoint the exact reason. Do you drop the ends of your words? Do you slur words together? Do you have trouble pronouncing a sound or a specific series of sounds? These can all be found by listening to your own voice recordings. Often, what you sound like in your head isn't how you sound to others, and the best way to find out what your voice sounds like is to listen to your recordings.
- However, realize everyone has a unique voice. You need to really embrace your voice and do the most you can with it; do not try to completely change it.

THE ELEVATOR PITCH

"You have 90 seconds, if you're lucky. If you can't make your point persuasively in that time, you've lost the chance for impact. Facts and figures are important, but it's not the only criteria, you must present in a manner that generates expertise and confidence." —Robert Herjavec

An elevator pitch is a short blurb that is between thirty and sixty seconds and will help get someone interested in your business. The name comes from the fact it is something you can say when you want to introduce your idea to someone while you guys are on an elevator. In fact, there is even a TV show made of people giving elevator pitches to investors while on the elevator (watch some episodes on YouTube to get a better idea of what an elevator pitch should sound like).

You can use this when meeting investors, trying to get people to support your cause, or just sharing your idea with someone you just met. If you attend any entrepreneurship events or competitions, this would be a great way to introduce your idea. Sean Wise, a successful venture capitalist, shares some advice he has after hearing over 20,000 elevator pitches.

The two main parts to a good elevator pitch are: the current problem and your solution to it.

Several things you should be sure to include are:

"**Irrefutable.** Your pitch is a statement about your company. You want to state who you are and what you do, to the point that no one can deny your claims.

Succinct. The pitch needs to be quick and easy, something you could say in one or two breaths.

Understandable. Everyone should be able to hear your pitch and get a proper snapshot of your company. No tech talk!

Attractive. You want to show the reward is worth the risk."

If you are pitching to an investor, you need to find a way to stand out. Chances are, they have been hearing business pitches all day, and you should do whatever you can to make your presentation memorable.

Here is a general template for an elevator pitch many entrepreneurs use:

1. Introduce yourself and your company.
2. Talk about what the problem is.
3. Explain how your company/idea/product will be the perfect solution.
4. Show how it has worked so far and how receptive buyers have been to it.
5. Somewhere in the pitch, work in a question that is either rhetorical or has a short answer in order to better engage the audience.
6. End with a call to action. When you do this, the audience knows exactly what to do if they are interested in your startup.

Toggl's blog, which provides all sorts of business and productivity advice, also gives another easy to remember template for an elevator pitch:

- Problem: "[Customer Type] are often frustrated by the effort it takes to [Action]."
- Solution: "[Your New Solution] eliminates the need to [Customer's Old Solution]."
- Why You: "For [Duration], [Customer Type] have trusted [Your Company] to provide the best solutions in [Customer's Industry]."
- Value: "With [Your New Solution], you can [spend less/make more] [time/money] [Action]."
- CTA: "I'll give you a call to learn more about your situation (Get Contact Info). Thanks for your time."

OTHER THINGS TO KEEP IN MIND

- Talk at a normal speed: although you are on a time crunch, it does not mean you should talk fast. Talking fast will make you hard to understand and make it even harder for whomever you are talking to, to absorb your message.
- Know your end goal: are you trying to get someone interested in joining your team or investing money? Different end goals require different startup pitches—don't prepare just one.
- Practice! Practice doesn't make perfect, but it can help you get a better idea of what you want to say in your elevator pitch.
- Make certain to convey how you are different from other companies that are doing similar things. Avoid jargon, buzzwords, and slang. Keep your pitch simple and understandable.
- Pitch decks are the presentation, often PowerPoints, that give a general overview of the venture, goals, and structure. If you are pitching to an investor, this is likely what you are going to be going off of. You can find the original

pitch decks of many successful startups (such as Airbnb) through a quick Google search. Use these as inspiration for your pitches!

TAKEAWAYS:

- Public speaking is an incredibly important skill you need to develop, even if you aren't too comfortable doing it right now.
- Being a great public speaker comes down to both practice and being in the right headspace.
- Prepare an elevator pitch in case you meet people who want to learn more about your social venture.

CONFIDENCE

"Most people live in a restricted circle of potential."

—WILLIAM JAMES

Imagine you are an investor. You have some money you are looking to put into the next big idea. How will you decide who to give it to?

Surprisingly, it may not be the person who actually has the greatest idea. Most of the time, whoever convinces the investor their idea is the greatest will get the funding. You need to make the investor believe one hundred percent that your project will succeed. What's more, you will need to make sure that the issue you are targeting becomes relevant to the investor. Let him know exactly how outrageous the problem is, and then show him how your idea will be the perfect solution. Even if you are not convinced your idea is the best, **convince your investor it is**.

So what exactly is confidence? Psychologists call it "self efficacy"—a person's belief they will be able to accomplish a goal. Confidence is strongly correlated with sticking to high goals you set for yourself, as well as bouncing back and persisting after failure. When you're confident, you are able to more accurately gauge your personal abilities.

Confidence can play a significant role in your success as a social entrepreneur. In many of my interviews with social entrepreneurs, they cited confidence as one of the qualities that they thought were the most important to entrepreneurial success. Francisco Dao, an organizational performance and strategy speaker, emphasizes the importance of confidence in being a good leader. He compares a lack of confidence to a house without a foundation, saying, "Trying to teach leadership without first building confidence is like building a house on a foundation of sand. It may have a nice coat of paint, but it is ultimately shaky at best. While the leadership community has focused on passion, communication, and empowerment, they've ignored this most basic element, and in the process they have planted these other components of leadership in a bed of quicksand."

A famous psychologist John Grohol explained that "People with a good and healthy self-esteem are able to feel good about themselves for who they are, appreciate their own worth, and take pride in their abilities and accomplishments. They also acknowledge that while they're not perfect and have faults, those faults don't play an overwhelming or irrationally large role in their lives or their own self-image." Being confident in your abilities and in your idea will allow you to see the entire situation more clearly, and thus, make decisions based on the actual situation as opposed to trying to prove your abilities and worth to others.

Confidence is also closely linked to passion for your business. Richard Branson notes, "Don't start a company unless it's an obsession and something you love, because if you have an exit strategy, it's not an obsession." When you are talking to others to get support for your business, a lack of passion for your cause is a clear turn off. This passion is essential for your venture's success. In an interview with Bill Gates, Warren Buffet claimed, "If you see somebody with even reasonable intelligence and a terrific passion for what they do and who can get people around them to march, even when those people can't see over the top of the next hill, things are gonna happen."

A study at the University of Melbourne found that confidence is a key determinate of workplace success. The researchers collected data from numerous large corporations in Melbourne, New York, and Toronto to assess the effect of confidence on career success. They discovered that those who self-reported higher levels of confidence earlier in their lives not only earned better wages, but also were promoted more often.

A couple helpful pointers suggested by that can help you come off as more confident are shared below. Keep in mind that confidence is less about your actual ability to succeed, but more about if you think you will, and that mindset in turn plays a role in your actual success.

1. Improve your posture. Bad posture can give off the impression that you are lazy and insecure. Numerous studies have shown that there is a very strong correlation between posture, brain functioning, mood, and energy levels. Sitting up straight will send a signal to your brain that you are confident and in charge of the situation. This is something that is not only easy to improve, but also can make a huge difference in how you look and how you feel.

2. Ditch the self-deprecation. Don't stress too much about how others might think of you. Negative thoughts can have a huge impact on your productivity and your ability to reach your full potential.

3. Take a minute every day to establish goals for the future. Jot them down somewhere. Studies have shown when you write something down, as opposed to just keeping it in your head, you are much more likely to accomplish it.

4. Stay positive! Be grateful! Positivity is contagious and will create a much better working environment.

5. Dress for the occasion. While dressing up isn't the number one concern when you are about to go in and pitch to investors, it is something that you should keep in mind to do the best you possibly can. No matter what you hear, first impressions matter. Make you sure what you wear aligns with the event or office dress code and values.

6. Don't sweat the small stuff. If you mess something up, apologize, accept your mistake, do your best to fix it, and move on.

7. Keep on learning. Always strive to improve, whether it is learning a new language or taking a class in a subject that interests you. These small accomplishments may serve as great confidence boosters.

8. Have fun. This sounds cliché, but make sure you take some time out of your day to do the things you love!
9. If you don't know something, ask for advice. People are more helpful than you think. In the next chapter, I talk a little more about how to find a mentor to help you through the process of launching your startup.
10. Slow down when you speak. When you are nervous, you automatically begin to talk faster, which may make you come off as scattered and unsure. Take a deep breath, practice good posture, and make sure you get your point across.
11. If you need to, fake it till you make it. Even if you aren't exactly sure about your idea or product, you need to convince others it is a great idea. In order to do this, you need to make it appear that you are one hundred percent behind your idea.[34]

Imagine you are at a leadership board meeting and you have come up with a set of goals you want to achieve in the next few weeks—let's say you want to expand your project or program into three more states by the end of the month. Now, based on the current circumstances of your organization, this is quite a far reach, but you think it could be possible with a little extra work. Now, whether you get this task done or not may largely depend on the confidence you show your team you have for this plan. If you say, "Hey guys, really should try to expand XYZ into three more states by the end of the month, but we don't know if you can," then the lack of confidence within that statement causes your team to doubt

---

34 Whitmore, Jacqueline. 2020. "9 Ways To Show More Confidence In Business". *Entrepreneur.*

what they are doing, which may lead to them falling short of the goal. On the other hand, if you say to you team, "We need to get into three more states by the end of the month! This will be easy to do, if you accomplish XYZ," then you sound much surer of what you are planning, which will ensure the team members are more motivated that their work will lead to this positive end goal.

However, with confidence, try your best to find a healthy level that doesn't step into the realm of narcissism. The Dunning-Kruger effect states that incompetent people can sometimes have the illusion of being more capable than they truly are. You probably know someone who in conversations, take a strong stance on something that they know little about, and rattle off opinions that are blatantly just uninformed and nonsense. That is a prime example of this effect, where someone think that they are much smarter than they actually are.

The key to avoiding this is developing a good sense of self-awareness and stepping back to take a look at your abilities.

FINDING
THE RIGHT MENTOR

———

Chances are, you probably haven't started something like this before. Instead of fumbling your way through figuring out how to handle the forms, find the right sources of funding, and market the organization, it is often very beneficial to find someone who has already taken the path you are.

A mentor can offer you many things to help guide you on your journey to create a successful social venture.

KNOWLEDGE OF THE INDUSTRY AND PROCESS

One of the most valuable things mentors can offer you is their knowledge and experiences. More than likely, they have already been through what you are going through right now and know the easiest and most effective way to get things done. Neil Robinson, the founder of a healthy chocolate company, expresses the invaluable experience having a mentor has provided him.

"I left my academic biomedical research position to launch my healthier chocolate company. Having no prior business experience, it was pretty obvious that I needed a mentor-there is so much of the business world that I just didn't know about. Having an experienced business mentor has been invaluable to the continued development of my company."

A good mentor who already knows the ropes can also offer advice as to how to successfully grow your startup so it can impact as many people as possible. For example, as a student, you probably don't know too much about marketing. However, with a mentor, they can help you find which advertising channels worked the best for them, and thus, may be beneficial for you to pursue.

If you just peruse online, there seem to be endless resources about how to start and grow a startup, but what is the most valuable is your mentor's personal experience in the environment you are in. This will allow you to develop a plan that is perfectly catered toward your business and not toward a cookie-cutter model that is shared on YouTube.

A strong mentorship has positively impacted numerous startups by helping them shape their goals and business plan.

Taylor and Steve Smith are two parents who after hearing about the tragic Sandy Hook school shooting in Connecticut, decided they needed to do whatever they could to help teachers be prepared for active shooter situations. The pair created Guardian Defense to allow teachers, the real first responders, to appropriately react in case an emergency occurs.

"Without prior experience operating a business, we have consulted greatly with our mentors on topics such as accounting, legal concerns, affiliations, partnerships, sales, grant writing, insurance, public speaking, employment and business management. Essentially, we show up with a list of questions seeking their guidance, and they are ready to answer!"

- consider joining an accelerator—there, you will be able to get funding and mentorship
- ask around—friends and family may know people in your industry
- get a LinkedIn to take advantage of your connections and your professional network.

There are several things you should keep in mind to find a mentor who will be the most helpful for you to grow your business. Timothy Arnoo, the founder of Fanbytes, shares tips for finding a great startup mentor.

1. Ask yourself: what do you really want to learn? After you find an answer, look for someone with these skills.
2. Find a mentor who is only a few steps ahead of you. As appealing as it would be to find a mentor that is an industry giant, chances are, they forgot many of the steps they had to go through when just starting up. Pinpoint what stage you are in the start-up process (if you are reading this, I'm assuming you haven't started yet or have just begun to come up with an idea). As Arnoo says, "Find that mentor that you wish to be in 3-5 years' time."
3. Make sure the relationship isn't entirely one sided. While your mentor will help provide you with valuable insights and tips, let them know you can help them provide a new

perspective on their business as well. This way, they are more inclined to help you.

WHERE TO FIND THEM

NETWORKING EVENTS

If you live near what is called an "entrepreneurship hot spot" such as Silicon Valley (in San Francisco, CA) or Crystal City (in Arlington, VA), there may be lots of incubators (places where startups can initially work and get ideas) nearby.

Even if your city isn't known for successful startups, chances are, there are some startup incubators in the area. Just search it up on Google and you'll probably find a couple. Another option would be to look for startup events or competitions in your area. Many universities host pitch competitions or hackathons for startups, which may be open to both students and the public. You can go into these and find a couple people to talk with and see if any of them can help you out or give you advice. There are also many Facebook groups for both entrepreneurship and social impact—joining these is also a great way to get to know more people in your field. Keep in mind, you don't necessarily need to find someone who can stick with you throughout the entire process. Any help or advice should be appreciated!

VOLUNTEERING

If you volunteer for an organization related to your cause, you'll likely meet people who are interested in creating change in the same thing you are. These would be great people to talk to about the issue you are addressing specifically and what their experience with dealing with it is.

LINKEDIN

I've mentioned this in another chapter as well, but it is extremely helpful to get a LinkedIn account. Almost everyone in the professional community has one, and it is a great way to reach someone who you find to have an interesting project that is related to yours. Make sure you use a nice looking profile photo and include your message when you send a connect request.

Once you do find a mentor, here are some things that you should keep in mind and be aware of:

- Be sure you are the one taking the initiative in asking for help; don't be annoying, but since your mentor is likely pretty busy, you should be the one scheduling meetings and asking questions. If you don't interact with your mentor enough early on, they won't be as inclined to stay in contact with and help you. Try to find specific things with which you need help. Sometimes a mentor will be eager to help but does not know what exactly you need.
- While a mentor is helpful, know they are not necessarily right one hundred percent of the time. Your idea/startup may be quite different from what your mentor was involved in, meaning their experiences may not always apply to yours. Listen, absorb, and evaluate your mentor's advice; however, don't treat is as absolute fact.

- Always be grateful! Make sure to send them a thank you email after they help you out with something significant, and don't forget to send a holiday card or gift.

PROGRAMS

As a student, there are a plethora of online programs and accelerators meant specifically to help young people make a difference in the community. You can find anything ranging from start-up competitions to grants to programs just offering to provide free mentorship to startups led by high school students. When filling out an application for one of these, make sure you have either a great idea or have done some sort of work to prove that your idea is viable.

When they are looking through applications, they are looking for not only great ideas, but also teams that have potential to succeed with a little extra help. Put a decent amount of work into writing a great application or grant and you may just end up with someone who can help you take the next step in your startup. Below are some good programs you could check out:

- Peacefirst
- LaunchX
- Startup Island
- Startup High School
- Quarter Zero

And more! Just do a quick Google search to see if more programs are available which are specific to your idea.

Finding a fitting mentor goes hand in hand with becoming more confident about your venture. Since your mentor can help you better develop a good plan and give you advice about what you are working on, you can become surer about your decisions, which will definitely be reflected in your confidence levels.

FINAL WORDS

——

So there you go. What you read was a summary of everything that I wish I've known since the beginning of high school about how to leverage your skills to create a social impact in a meaningful and exciting way. I'm sure a lot of you are involved in all sorts of volunteer activities, which may be great! I'm not saying that you should just drop all those things, but make sure you take a step back and consider the impact of the work and the time that you are putting in. If you feel that what you're doing is helping a lot of people in an effective way, by all means, continue doing it. The last thing I want to do is come off as dissing volunteering, but just make sure that you are committing your time to creating something that you enjoy and are proud of.

Social entrepreneurship is a pretty recent approach on creating community impact, and has proven itself to be a catalyst for social change. After spending hundreds of hours talking to people and doing research, here are some points that I hope you walk away with:

- Make sure that you commit to a cause that you are truly passionate about and know you can stick with through all sorts of challenges that creating a start-up will throw your way.
- Take some time each day to analyze successful people around you. Who do you admire? Is there someone that you aspire to become? Now go see if they have any advice! Make it a goal to pick up some good habits and traits. Learn about and connect with interesting social entrepreneurs.
- When you're creating a social venture, thoroughly research the industry, as well as other companies that are doing similar things. This may prevent you from having an "oops I tried to solve the completely wrong problem" moment two years into your project.
- There are a lot of skills such as finding funding, networking, or hosting events that you might not have initially, but will definitely pick up along the way. Learn from successes. Learn from failures. Make sure to take the entire process as a learning experience!

Whether or not you have something you are already working on, creating a successful social venture will undoubtedly take a lot of time and effort. However, if you are up for it, this is the perfect time to jump into this industry and make a difference.

Now go out there and change the world!

BIBLIOGRAPHY

———

2019. *Terracycle.*

"5 Tips To Help You Find Your Passion". 2020. *Forbes.Com.*

"10 Key Characteristics Of A Successful Entrepreneur". 2020. *Life-hack.*

"Andrew Carnegie". 2020. *Biography.*

"Barbara Corcoran Official Website". 2020. *Barbara Corcoran.*

"Bill & Melinda Gates Foundation". 2020. *Bill & Melinda Gates Foundation.*

"Communicate Your Message Effectively—The Number One Fear". 2019. *Westsidetoastmasters.Com.*

"Elon Musk | Tesla". 2020. *Tesla.Com.*

"Executive Team | Patriot Software". 2020. *Patriot Software.*

"Grameen Bank". 2020. *Grameen Bank—Bank For The Poor.*

Henricks, Mark. 2019. "Do You Really Need A Business Plan?". *Entrepreneur.*

Henricks, Mark. 2020. "Do You Really Need A Business Plan?". *Entrepreneur.*

"History". 2019. *Grameenfoundation.Org*. "How Sam Polk, Former Wall Street Trader And 'Wealth Addict,' Broke Free Of His Golden Handcuffs". 2020. *Forbes.Com*.

"How The Flora App Developers Use Behavioral Psychology To Help Users Live Their Best Lives | Designli Blog". 2020. *Designli Blog*.

"How To Build A Team That Won't Sink Your Startup". 2020. *Neil Patel*.

"Huffpost Is Now A Part Of Verizon Media". 2020. *Huffpost.Com*.

improvepresentation.com, What. 2019. "What Is A Pitch Deck—Pitch Deck Template". *Pitchdeck.Improvepresentation.Com*. "Jimmy Fallon". 2020. *Biography*.

"John D. Rockefeller". 2020. *HISTORY*."Mark Cuban". 2020. *Biography*."Mark Zuckerberg—Facebook, Family & Facts—Biography". 2020. *Biography.Com*. "Microsoft Founded". 2020. *HISTORY*. Mycoskie, Blake. 2019. "How I Did It: The TOMS Story". *Entrepreneur*.

Neely, Joe. 2019. "Top 7 Killer Elevator Pitch Examples—Toggl Blog". *Toggl Blog*.

"Negotiations". 2020. *Hbr.Org*.

"Okrs". 2020. *Medium*.

"Our Stories—Google". 2020. *About.Google*.

"Richard". 2020. *Virgin*.

Rosenburg, Stephanie. 2020. "Volunteering: History Of An American Value | Engaging Volunteers". *Engaging Volunteers*. Schreier, Hannah M. C., Kimberly A. Schonert-Reichl, and Edith Chen. 2013. "Effect Of Volunteering On Risk Factors For Cardiovascular Disease In Adolescents". *JAMA Pediatrics* 167 (4): 327. doi:10.1001/jamapediatrics.2013.1100.

"Self-Confidence The Secret To Workplace Advancement". 2019. *Sciencedaily*. "Sharing Research On Failure And Education Globally". 2020. *Teachers College—Columbia University.*

"Social Entrepreneurship: 7 Ways To Empower Student Change-makers". 2019. *Edutopia.*

"Tap The Power Of Storytelling". 2019. *Forbes.Com.* "The Buried Life". 2020. *The Buried Life.* "The Growth Mindset—What Is Growth Mindset—Mindset Works". 2020. *Mindsetworks.Com.*

"The Invention Of The Baby Carrot". 2020. *Priceonomics.*

"The Paypal Mafia". 2020. *Fortune.*

"The TOMS Story | TOMS®". 2020. *Toms.Com.*

Truong, Florina. 2019. "Why Schools Should Teach Entrepreneurship". *Entrepreneur.*

"'What's An Entrepreneur?' Here's The Best Answer Ever". 2020. *Inc.Com.*

Whitmore, Jacqueline. 2020. "9 Ways To Show More Confidence In Business". *Entrepreneur.*

"Why It'S Imperative To Teach Entrepreneurship". 2020. *Medium.*

"William Drayton". 2020. *Ashoka | Everyone A Changemaker.*

Wise, Sean. 2019. "I've Heard 20,000 Elevator Pitches. Here's What They've Taught Me About Getting Funded". *Inc.Com.*